The Priesthood of The Apocalypse:

The 144 Thousand

By: Evangelist Larry E. Wolfe
http://www.btmi.org

The Priesthood of the Apocalypse
The 144 Thousand
By: Evangelist Larry E. Wolfe

ISBN 978-0-578-02168-3

All rights reserved.
Written permission must be secured from the author to transmit or reproduce any part of this book, by any means electronic or mechanical, except for brief quotations in critical reviews or articles. All copyright information must be included with any quotations.

Unless otherwise specified, all Scripture quotations are based on the Authorized King James Version
Copyright 2009 by: Evangelist Larry E. Wolfe

For more information visit: www.btmi.org
Printed in the United States of America
First Edition, April 2009

INTRODUCTION

The study of the prophetic Scriptures in recent years has escalated as recorded by Daniel the prophet:
"Seal the book even to the time of the end: many shall run to and fro and knowledge shall be increased...And he said, Go thy way Daniel: for the words are closed up and sealed till the time of the end." (Daniel 12:4, 9)

Daniel's prophecy of the heightened activity of those who *"shall run to and fro"* refers to this increased study of his writings and the other prophetic Scriptures that are tied to his book. The result is *"knowledge shall be increased"* when God opens up those truths that were formerly *"closed up and sealed till the time of the end."*

"The Priesthood of the Apocalypse" is an examination of these Scriptures focusing upon The 144 Thousand who are unfolded in the prophetic Word as they are the necessary continuation of the priesthood of believers *after* the rapture of the saints during the time of God's wrath which is called the Day of the Lord.

This study lays emphasis upon the literal method of interpreting the Scripture for the plain common sense interpretation provides the most accurate rendering as the following quote underlines:
"Many of the interpretations placed upon the Bible's revelation of the future presuppose that it just cannot mean what the words plainly seem to say, therefore, another explanation is required. That is the common source of the alternative prophetic views. Men come to the Bible and look at prophecy. Ideas have come to them from various quarters, and they admit that, at the first reading, they would understand these words simply to mean one thing, yet they maintain that the words do not mean what they plainly appear to say. That is unbelief. That is, we need someone to interpret for us what God has said, and that makes the interpreter the authority, not God. If someone speaks to me in a foreign language and I have another to interpret, I utterly depend on what the interpreter tells me. Thus, when prophetic teachers say what God means when He has said something different,

we would have to trust in them, and not in what the Bible says if we accept such adjusting of the plain language of God. That is the problem source. That is the common pattern in all of the alternative prophetic views that are to be found amongst God's people, an alternative to the simple understanding that what God says is precisely what He means." ("A Correct Understanding of Pre-Millennial Truth-An Aid to Faith" pp.19 "Watching and Waiting" by: Ivan Foster)

By utilizing the literal method of interpretation, the Scriptures take on new meaning in passages that have controlled the prophetic thinking of many of those who are Bible believers. The focus of this study centers upon The 144 Thousand who are God's lifeline to those who will be saved during the time after the saints are raptured. They will be sealed for protection (Revelation 7:1-8; 9:4) in order to continue their ministry (Revelation 14:1-5) during the Day of the Lord when God pours out His wrath upon earth.

They also appear in the Old Testament (Psalm 110; Obadiah; Micah 5) providing additional information illuminating their coming ministry during a time when the earth will be experiencing the most devastating and destructive judgments from the Lord as described in Revelation 8-19. "The Priesthood of the Apocalypse" unfolds the vital Redemption Ministry of The 144 Thousand who will be God's kingdom of priests on earth during the Day of the Lord.

Table of Contents

Chapter	Description	Page
1.	The 144 Thousand's Ministry Overview	7
2.	The 144 Thousand's Source: The 12 Tribes	24
3.	The 144 Thousand's Supernatural Calling	37
4.	The Passing of the Torch: Part I	41
5.	The Passing of the Torch: Part II	48
6.	The Passing of the Torch: Part III	55
7.	The 144 Thousand Soldiers	58
8.	The 144 Thousand Saviors	66
9.	The Priesthood of the Apocalypse: Part I	69
10.	The Priesthood of the Apocalypse: Part II	88
11.	The Purpose of God	117
12.	The Author's Background	131

The 144 Thousand
Ministry Overview

In Revelation 7:1-8 the New Testament introduces a most significant group of *"servants of our God" (Revelation 7:3)* also known as the 144 Thousand Sons of Israel.

They are from the twelve tribes of Israel and are sealed by the name of the Father and the name of the Lamb which are written on their foreheads (Revelation 7:3-8, 14:1).

These choice servants are somewhat of a mystery, especially concerning their end of the age purpose and spiritual condition at the time of their sealing. The actual time of their sealing is clearly fixed for it immediately follows the sign of the Second Coming of Christ and the Day of the Lord (Matthew 24:29-31; Revelation 6:12-17).

They are sealed by God's signature just before Christ's Coming occurs (Revelation 7:9-17; Matthew 24:30, 31) and the Day of the Lord begins (Revelation 8:1, 2). The Church saints who have been *"sealed [by the Holy Spirit] unto the day of redemption"*
(Ephesians 4:30) will be raptured when He comes.

The day of redemption refers to the day the rapture occurs, for the Church saints will not experience the great and dreadful Day of the Lord's wrath (I Thessalonians 1:9, 5:10). But, the 144 Thousand, who are sealed by the signature of God (Revelation 14:1) will be protected and remain active on earth, serving the Lord, after the rapture during the Day of the Lord (Revelation 9:4, 14:1-5, 17:14).

Just before the Church saints are raptured, they will "Pass the Torch" as it were, to these 144 Thousand servants of God in order that the priesthood of believers and testimony of the Lord Jesus Christ continue throughout the coming Day of the Lord.

This Redemption Ministry in effect will be their primary charge during the Day of the Lord when they will evangelize those Jews (Daniel 11:32-35, 12:3) and Gentiles (Isaiah 19:16-25; Micah 7:15-17) whom God will redeem during that future time of judgment upon the earth.

One of the important questions concerning the 144 Thousand is their spiritual condition at the time they are sealed, and there are only two options, are they saved or unsaved when they are sealed? This significant group of young men, the 144 Thousand *"of all the tribes of the children [sons] of Israel" (Revelation 7:4),* are physically marked by the Lord.

Although there are others upon whom the Lord puts His mark described in the pages of Scripture, this group, appearing numerous times in the Word of God, is the most notable. They are called *"servants of our God"* **before** they are sealed and as the end times are studied they also appear a number of other places supplying indicators of their spiritual condition at the time they are sealed in Revelation 7:3-8.

Determining the exact point in time that they are sealed is also important to note in order to discern just exactly what it is that the Lord has for them to accomplish. The text isolates their sealing by utilizing time indicating phrases to set off this major event: *"And after these things" (Revelation 7:1), "After this" (Revelation 7:9),* demonstrating the uniqueness and importance of what takes place between these two phrases.

Their sealing occurs immediately after the sign of the Second Coming of Christ and the Day of the Lord (Revelation 6:12-6:17; Joel 2:30, 31) and just before the Rapture of the saints (Revelation 7:9-7). Both of these events occur on *"the same day"* as taught by the Lord in Luke 17:22-37. The Lord will surely deliver the saints **before** He initiates His wrath-filled judgment just as He has done in the past and just as He promised to do in the future (I Thessalonians 1:10, 5:9).

Therefore, the 144 Thousand will be sealed just before the Day of the Lord begins since they appear with the Lord Jesus Christ later, during the Day of the Lord in Revelation 14:1-5, 17:14. They also are referred to in Revelation 9:4 and 12:17 with all of these texts supplying additional information concerning this key end of the age kingdom of priests.

Their background prior to their sealing must be considered for they most certainly will have paths similar to those other servants listed throughout the Old and New Testaments. This question must be answered: "Are they saved before or after they are sealed?" Although it surely is possible that they are not saved before they are sealed, it is highly unlikely for a number of reasons.

First of all they are called *"servants of our God" (Revelation 7:3)* which is a title reserved for those who have attained a certain level of spiritual maturity and dedication to the Lord:
"The Revelation of Jesus Christ which God gave unto Him to show unto His servants things which must shortly come to pass." (Revelation 1:1)

This opening verse designates a group of people to whom the Lord Jesus Christ would *"show"* His vital end of the age truths contained in the Apocalypse, and that group of people are called *"His servants"* (Revelation 1:1). His servants include select men and women who were and are willing to *"spend and be spent" (II Corinthians 12:15)* for the cause and glory of the Lord Jesus Christ.

This word translated servant is the Greek word *"doulos"* meaning bondservant or slave, indicating one who is totally given over to the will of his master. It is found in the New Testament over 120 times. There are a number of different Greek words translated servant in the King James Version with various meanings such as attendant, minister, household worker, hired employee and under rower. But, the one the Lord chose to describe the 144 Thousand is the Greek word *"doulos"* which refers to the ultimate servant with respect to the total giving of themselves to the service of their master.

This is the word used by the Apostle Paul to describe his own position in relationship to his Lord a number of times (Romans 1:1; Philippians 1:1; Titus 1:1). The epistles reveal the "doulos" or "servants of the Lord Jesus Christ" also include Timothy, Epaphras, Peter, James, John, and Jude.

In the book of the Revelation the same word also describes Moses and the prophets as servants of God (Revelation 10:7, 15:3). But, the most significant occurrences of this word describe the Lord Jesus Christ Himself:

*"Behold, My **Servant** Whom I have chosen, My Beloved in Whom My soul is well pleased, I will put My Spirit upon Him and He will show judgment to the Gentiles." (Matthew 12:18)*

*"Let this mind be in you which was also in Christ Jesus: Who, being in the form of God, thought it not robbery to be equal with God: But made Himself of no reputation, and took upon Him the form of a **servant** and was made in the likeness of men." (Philippians 2:5-7)*

Those *"servants of our God"*, or bond-slaves of God, in Revelation 7:3 must also be considered to be of this same Biblically defined caliber:

*"Hurt not the earth till we have sealed the **servants** of our God in their foreheads. And I heard the number of them which were sealed an hundred and forty and four thousand of all the tribes of the children of Israel." (Revelation 7:3, 4)*

These 144 Thousand Sons of Israel are definitely classified as *"doulos"* or bondservants along with the Lord, and those Apostles and other saints used mightily of the Lord. This specific word was chosen by the Holy Spirit to describe this select group of men in order to indicate their advanced spiritual condition and relationship to God at the time they are sealed, for they are called *"the servants of our God"* by the angel **before** they are sealed.

This unique group of God's servants are key end times saints and some of the most thoroughly described people in the Word of God. They are seen or referred to in Psalm 110, the book of Daniel 11:32-35, 12:3, 10; Obadiah 17-21; and the book of the Revelation of Jesus Christ: 7:1-8, 9:4, 12:17, 14:1-5, 17:14, 19:19.

Secondly, their decision to be *"undefiled by women" (Revelation 14:4)* reveals their level of dedication to the Lord early in manhood, prior to their sealing. This major decision indicates that they are men of God who have set themselves apart having discerned a certain calling of God upon their lives prior to making this important decision for Christ.

They literally will give up the natural desire to marry and have a wife and children in order to give themselves totally to the Lord. By doing this they will greatly limit the effect sexual temptation can have upon their lives and thereby remove the ever increasing pressure from the world, the flesh and the devil to fall into sex sin.

Also, remaining unmarried will give them additional opportunity for focused service to the Lord as clearly recommended and practiced by the Apostle Paul (I Corinthians 7:8, 26, 32).

Number three, and definitely one of the most compelling affirmations concerning their spiritual condition at their sealing, is revealed by asking this question: "Would God literally put His name and the name of His Son, The Lamb (Revelation 14:1) upon someone who is an unbelieving depraved sinner, not having experienced Bible salvation by grace through faith in the Blood of Christ?"

The answer to this question must be a definite NO! In addition to these three facts indicating their spiritual condition at the time they are sealed, there are three other Bible examples of the Lord putting His identification or mark upon men:
"Him that overcomes will I make a pillar in the temple of My God, and he shall go no more out: and I will write upon him the name of My God and the name of the city of My God, which is new Jerusalem, which cometh down out of heaven from My God: and I will write upon him My new name." (Revelation 3:12)

These over-comers of the church of Philadelphia are given five blessed promises by the Lord Jesus Christ reserved for those who attain an overcoming level of victory during their time on earth:
1. *I will make him a pillar in the temple of My God*
2. *He shall go no more out [remains in the temple]*
3. *I will write upon him the name of My God*
4. *I will write upon him the name of the city of My God, which is new Jerusalem*
5. *I will write upon him My new name.*

These saints are promised some of the most valuable and

privileged rewards ever spoken of in the Scripture. Being a pillar in the heavenly temple of Jehovah rings of a highly exalted heavenly position, however, this reward is given the added blessing of being eternal.

These over-comers will have three different inscriptions upon them and not one of them is trivial. All three are truly to be cherished for the incomparable recognition given to those who overcome during their days upon earth, for these names are the three most honorable identities in all of heaven.

The next example is found in the last chapter of the book of Revelation:
"And there shall be no more curse: but the throne of God and of the Lamb shall be in it; and His servants shall serve Him: And they shall see His face; and His name shall be in their foreheads."
(Revelation 22:3, 4)

Notice, these glorified servants of God have the honored privilege of seeing the face of the Lord Jesus Christ, and they also will have the Lamb's name in their foreheads, similar to the 144 Thousand. However, the 144 Thousand have both the Father's name and the name of the Lamb in their foreheads (Revelation 14:1) showing their dual branches of service, being *"servants of our God" (Revelation 7:3)* while also physically serving on earth *"with"* the Lamb during the Day of the Lord. (Revelation 14:1-5, 17:14, 19:19).

In these two instances, the over-comers of the church in Philadelphia and the servants in glory, both having God's identification, are clearly believers, fully redeemed, belonging to the Lord. In order for the Lord to put His name on men, it is evident by these passages that they are definitely children of God when they receive this glorious inscription upon them.

This sets a high standard by which to measure these 144 Thousand sons of Israel, for they will be given God's identification when they are still mere mortals. This underlines the significance of the Lord's bestowal of His signature upon those whom He knows will be worthy of His name during their apocalyptic priesthood in the Day of the Lord.

In Ezekiel's vision of chapter nine a third example is recorded:
"And the Lord said unto him, Go through the midst of the city, through the midst of Jerusalem, and set a mark upon the foreheads of the men that sigh and that cry for all the abominations that be done in the midst thereof." (Ezekiel 9:4)

These men who are marked by God are those who openly express their disgust and sorrow over the sinful condition of Jerusalem demonstrating their allegiance to the Lord. They are given God's saving protection from the impending slaughter of His coming judgment (Ezekiel 9:1-11).

These marked saints in Ezekiel are similar to the 144 Thousand for those who have His seal in their foreheads in that day will also be spared from God's judgment during the Day of the Lord:
"And it was commanded them [locusts] that they should not hurt the grass of the earth, neither any green thing, neither any tree; but only those men which have not the seal of God in their foreheads." (Revelation 9:4)

The information above indicates the 144 Thousand are surrendered saints who have duly earned their title as *"servants of our God"* before they are sealed. They have willingly surrendered themselves to the Lord to be sealed just prior to the Day of the Lord having become mature believers before that time, being worthy to have the holy name of the Father and the Lamb written in their foreheads.

This seal not only provides protection, but the seal can also indicate ownership, for these men have unconditionally and sacrificially given themselves to their Master for His service. Approximately when they are redeemed is indicated in Revelation 14:3, 4:
"The hundred and forty four thousand, which were redeemed from the earth." (Revelation 14:3)

The Greek participle translated *"which were redeemed"* is in the perfect tense indicating their redemption has already taken place at a given point in the past with continuing effect into the present. The act of redemption is not continuing, but the results of this past action of redemption are continuing.

The 144 Thousand are shown to be *"redeemed from the earth...redeemed from among men"* the two phrases indicating:
1. Where they are from: The earth
2. What they are: Men, from among men

They are not heavenly angelic beings. They are in fact men of like passions as we are, whom God will raise up from across the planet just as He has raised up His faithful servants throughout the history of mankind.

The second time the word *"redeemed"* appears (Revelation 14:4) it is a verb in the aorist tense, which indicates a completed action at one point in past time. The mood of this verb is passive indicating the act of redemption was not accomplished by those who were redeemed but by someone else, namely the Lord.

They are also entitled *"the first-fruits"* showing they are the first of an additional "more of the same" [Jews from the twelve tribes] future harvest who also will be *"redeemed from the earth...redeemed from among men"*. This oft-quoted verse specifies those Jews of this future harvest:
"When all Israel shall be saved: as it is written, There shall come out of Zion the Deliverer [Redeemer], and shall turn away ungodliness from Jacob." (Romans 11:26)

This future national redemption is the very event being celebrated in Revelation 14:1-3 at the end of the 70th Week of Daniel (Revelation 11:15). In addition, there are other Jews who are saved and remain on earth after the rapture, namely *"the two witnesses"* of Revelation 11 and *"the woman"* [Faithful Israel] of Revelation 12.

These saints will also continue on earth throughout the last 3-1/2 years of Daniel's 70th Week as the rapture occurs some time after the mid-point of this seven year period, but before the beginning of God's wrath which is the Day of the Lord.

This prophetic timeline is the Lord Jesus Christ's end of the age chronology found in Matthew 24:3-31, which shows the rapture (Matthew 24:30, 31) shortening the Great Tribulation (Matthew 24:29a) followed by the sign of the Second Coming of Christ and the impending Day of the Lord (Matthew 24:29b).

"The woman" [Faithful Israel] also is supernaturally protected during this time:
"And the woman fled into the wilderness where she hath a place prepared of God, that they should feed her there a thousand two hundred and threescore days. And to the woman were given two wings of a great eagle, that she might fly into the wilderness, into her place, where she is nourished for a time, and times, and half a time, from the face of the serpent." (Revelation 12:6, 14)

"The two witnesses" are eventually killed by the beast [the Antichrist] and ascend up to heaven after *"they shall have finished their testimony" (Revelation 11:7).* However, they also will continue on earth after the rapture to fulfill God's designated purpose during their supernatural 3-1/2 year ministry as mighty instruments of the judgment of God (Revelation 11:3-14).

The Lord rejoices in showing His mercy, and these 144 Thousand *"servants of our God"* will be His instruments of mercy during the end times as foretold in Daniel 11:32-35, 12:3, 10. They are seen as those who have insight and understanding instructing the many, being purged and purified during their Redemption Ministry.

This notable time of the end group of saints in Daniel 11 also appear after the mid-point of Daniel's 70th Week after the abomination of desolation is set up:
"And arms [forces] shall stand on his [the Antichrist] part, and they shall pollute the sanctuary of strength, and shall take away the daily sacrifice, and they shall place the abomination that makes desolate. And such as do wickedly against the covenant shall he corrupt by flatteries; but the people that do know their God shall be strong and do exploits. And they that understand among the people [Jews] shall instruct many: yet they shall fall by the sword, and by flame, by captivity, and by spoil, many days. And some of them understanding shall fall, to try them, and to purge, and to make them white, even to the time of the end: because it is yet for a time appointed."
(Daniel 11:31-33, 35)

At the beginning of the 70th Week *"[the] many"* Jews

(Daniel 9:27) will *"confirm the covenant"* with the Antichrist. These Jews will be thoroughly deceived, not knowing they are in fact consenting to *"a covenant with death" (Isaiah 28:15)* which will eventually bring about their destruction.

There will be those who are instructed by the 144 Thousand, those *"that understand among the people" (Daniel 11:33)* and they will *"turn many to righteousness"* who will receive the Messiah, the Lord Jesus Christ as their Savior:
"And they that be wise shall shine as the brightness of the firmament; and they that turn many to righteousness as the stars for ever and ever." (Daniel 12:3)

Those Jews who continue on in darkness will eventually *"forsake the holy covenant" (Daniel 11:30)* taking *"the mark... of the beast" (Revelation 13:17)* during the time of Satan's *"great wrath"* (Revelation 12:12), which is also referred to as *"great tribulation"* (Matthew 24:21). They will subsequently die during the Day of the Lord's wrath:
"And it shall come to pass, that in all the land, saith the Lord, two parts therein shall be cut off and die." (Zechariah 13:8a).

The prophet continues:
"But the third part shall be left therein. And I will bring the third part through the fire, and will refine them as silver is refined, and will try them as gold is tried: they shall call on My name, and I will hear them: I will say, It is My people: and they shall say, The LORD is My God." (Zechariah 13:8b, 9)

These of Zechariah's *"third part"* are those of Daniel's *"many"* who will be instructed by the 144 Thousand:
*"The people that do know their God...they that understand among the people...they that be wise...they that turn **many** to righteousness...the wise shall understand." (Daniel 11:32, 33; 12:3, 10)*

After the abomination of desolation, at the mid-point of Daniel's 70th Week, God has not yet sealed the 144 Thousand but they are among those in Israel referred to in the above Daniel passages and will successfully minister to the many unsaved.

This same group of Jews is evident continuing in the land after *"the woman"* flees into the wilderness:
"And the dragon [Satan] was wroth with the woman, and went to make war with the remnant [rest] of her seed, which keep the commandments of God, and have the testimony of Jesus Christ."
(Revelation 12:17b

The *"remnant of her seed"* indicated here refers to the rest of her physical seed, those Jews who remain in the land after the faithful (most likely: women, children, and men too old to go to war) flee into the wilderness. Their spiritual credentials are given in the last part of the verse: *"which keep the commandments of God, and have the testimony of Jesus Christ"*.

These Jews who remain in the land, *"the rest of her seed"*, will be these chosen men:
"Thy people shall be willing in the day of Thy power [Day of the Lord], in the beauties of holiness from the womb of the morning: Thou hast the dew of Thy youth [young men]/" (Psalm 110:3)

These are those priest/warriors of the Messiah, who will be part of the physical army of Israel who defend the land against the Antichrist when he first enters Israel. He makes war with the Jews as described in Micah 5:4-9 where those who remain are called *"the remnant of Jacob" (Micah 5:7, 8)*.

Some of them will be martyred or taken captive by the Antichrist: *"many days...even to the time of the end" (Daniel 11:35)*. This refers to the duration of the Great Tribulation being cut short when Christ comes to resurrect/rapture/rescue/receive the saints (Matthew 24:21-31; I Thessalonians 4:13-18; Revelation 7:9-17).

The 144 Thousand will continue into the Day of the Lord being *"purged and purified"* eventually being *"made white and tried" (Daniel 11:35, 12:10)*. It is at this point in time that the most prophesied event in Scripture begins, *"the great and dreadful day of the Lord' (Malachi 4:5)*.

This event in God's program is also referred to as *"the end"* by the Lord (Matthew 24:6, 14) and *"the time of the end...end of days"* by

Daniel (Daniel 11:35, 40, 12:4, 9, 13) both indicating the very same point in time.

It is on this day that God's prophetic *"time of the end"* program takes a major turn from the Antichrist's vicious persecution of God's people during the Great Tribulation to the Lord's Second Coming in glory:
"And then shall that wicked [Antichrist] be revealed whom the Lord will consume with the spirit of His mouth, and shall destroy [render powerless] with the brightness of His coming." (II Thessalonians 2:8)

It is on this same day, the sign of the Second Coming/Day of the Lord is given, (Revelation 6:12-17), the 144 Thousand are sealed (Revelation 7:1-8) and the Lord returns to rescue/receive (John 14:3) His saints by rapture (I Thessalonians 4:13-18), receiving them into heaven (Revelation 7:9-17).

The Lord will first seal and secure His servants, the 144 Thousand, before He rescues the saints with the sign of the Day of the Lord being given as a marvelous heavenly prelude to it all. These events will all occur the same day just as the Lord Jesus Christ taught when He emphasized *"**the same day**"* rescue before the retribution of God's judgment:
*"For as the lightning, that lightens out of the one part under heaven, shines unto the other part under heaven; so shall also the Son of man be in His day. But first He must suffer many things, and be rejected of this generation. And as it was in the days of Noah, so shall it be also in the days of the Son of man. They did eat, they drank, they married wives, they were given in marriage, until **the day** that Noah entered into the ark, and the flood came, and destroyed them all. Likewise, also as it was in the days of Lot; they did eat, they drank, they bought, they sold, they planted, they built; But **the same day** that Lot went out of Sodom it rained fire and brimstone from heaven, and destroyed them all. Even thus shall it be in **the day** when the Son of man is revealed." (Luke 17:24-30)*

Paul describes this same time just prior to the Day of the Lord:
"But of the times and seasons, brethren, ye have no need that I write unto you. For yourselves know perfectly that the day of the Lord so comes as a thief in the night. For when they [unsaved] shall say peace

and safety; then sudden destruction comes upon them and they shall not escape." (I Thessalonians 5:1, 2)

Although the Antichrist will come on his *"white horse"* as the end times world ruler *"conquering, and to conquer...taking peace from the earth...having a pair of balances"(Revelation 6:1-6)* and in the process will implement worldwide economic control, there will be a time of *"peace and safety"* just prior to the Day of the Lord when a "business as usual" attitude will prevail among the lost.

At this same time, persecution of the saints will reach the maximum level ever recorded in history (Matthew 24:15-28; Revelation 6:7-11). Then God will send His Son, the Lord Jesus Christ, to rescue/rapture the saints who have been *"sealed with that Holy Spirit of promise...unto the day of redemption" (Ephesians 1:13, 4:30).* Those whom He chooses to remain on earth will also be protected from His wrath just as He promised (Revelation 3:10, 9:4).

The 144 Thousand will be protected by having the name of the Father and the Lamb on their foreheads (Revelation 14:1), while the faithful of Israel [the woman] will be safe in *"a place prepared by God" (Revelation 12:6)* during the last 3-1/2 years of the 70th Week of Daniel.

She will *"fly into the wilderness" (Revelation 12:14)* and remain there until the end of the 70th Week. Eventually they will become the core group, along with the 144 Thousand and those of Israel who will be saved at the end of the 70th Week, who will populate the Promised Land during Christ's earthly 1000-year rule, called the Millennium (Revelation 20:1-10).

This protection during judgment by God is similar to the time when He brought the plagues upon Egypt and the Israelites were given safety in the land of Goshen while Moses and Aaron were actively confronting Pharaoh as the instruments of God's judgment.

Like Moses and Aaron, the two witnesses will serve as God's instruments of judgment (Revelation 11:3-7) during this unparalleled period of destruction which God brings upon the earth and its inhabitants, the cataclysmic Day of the Lord as described in

Revelation 8-11, 15-19.

While Moses and Aaron were the instruments of God's judgment to the lost and also the instruments of God's mercy to His people, the time of the end will see these same actions performed by *"the two witnesses' (Revelation 11:3-14)* and the 144 Thousand Sons of Israel.

God will continue to extend His eternal mercy to mankind through His 144 Thousand human servants just as He has done throughout the ages past. His primary purpose for the Day of the Lord is to purge and purify His people Israel; those referred to in Daniel 9:27, 11:33, 35, 12:3, 10. This time of the end purpose of God has also been foretold in other Old Testament prophecies: (Isaiah 1:24-28, 27:9; Jeremiah 30:7; Ezekiel 7:16-27; Zechariah 13:8, 9; Malachi 3:1-3).

His second purpose is the rightful judgment of planet earth and its unbelieving inhabitants who throughout all of the supernatural devastation, death and wholesale destruction repeatedly reject the Lord Jesus Christ by refusing to repent:
*"And the rest of the men which were not killed by these plagues yet repented not of the works of their hands, that they should not worship devils, and idols of gold, and silver, and brass, and stone, and of wood; which neither can see, nor hear nor walk: **Neither repented they** of their murders, nor of their sorceries, nor of their fornication, nor of their thefts." (Revelation 9:20, 21)*

*"And the fourth angel poured out his vial upon the sun; and power was given unto him to scorch men with fire. And men were scorched with great heat, and blasphemed the name of God, which hath power over these plagues: and they repented not to give Him glory. And the fifth angel poured out his vial upon the seat of the beast; and his kingdom was full of darkness; and they gnawed their tongues for pain. And blasphemed the God of heaven because of their pains and their sores, and **repented not** of their deeds." (Revelation 16:8-11)*

However, many Jews will turn to the Lord during this time, for the Lord will surely fulfill His promise:
"And it shall come to pass, that in all the land, saith the Lord, two parts therein shall be cut off and die; but the third shall be left therein. And I will bring the third part through the fire, and will refine

*them as silver is refined, and will try them as gold is tried: they shall **call** on My name, and I will hear them: I will say, It is My people: and they shall say, **The Lord is my God**." (Zechariah 13:8, 9)*

*"For whosoever shall **call** on the name of the Lord shall be saved. How then shall they **call** on Him in whom they have not **believed**? And how shall they **believe** on Him of whom they have not heard? And how shall they hear without a preacher? And how shall they preach, except they be sent? As it is written how beautiful are the feet of them that preach the Gospel of peace, and bring glad tidings of good things." (Romans 10:13-15)*

*"And I will show wonders in the heavens and in the earth, blood, and fire, and pillars of smoke. The sun shall be turned into darkness, and moon into blood, before the great and the terrible day of the Lord come. And it shall come to pass, that whosoever shall **call** upon the name of the LORD shall be delivered: for in mount Zion and in Jerusalem shall be deliverance, as the Lord hath said, and in the remnant whom the Lord shall call." (Joel 2:30-32)*

*"And the Redeemer shall come to Zion, and unto them that **turn** from transgression in Jacob, saith the Lord." (Isaiah 59:20)*

*"And so all Israel shall be saved: as it is written, There shall come out of Zion the Deliverer, and **shall turn away ungodliness** from Jacob: For this is My covenant unto them, when I **shall take away their sins.**" (Romans 11:26, 27)*

These Scriptures clearly show God's plan of salvation in the future deliverance of His people continues to operate just as it has in the past and present. Those whom He calls respond by believing, turning and calling upon Him in order to be saved from their sin. The entire work of salvation is of the Lord as He alone has the ability to *"turn away ungodliness from Jacob...when I shall take away their sins"*. *(Romans 11:26)*

God will send His end times kingdom of priests, the 144 Thousand sealed *"servants of our God"*, to His people so that those whom He calls will be able to hear, believe, turn and call on His name. They will be redeemed when they see their Redeemer, the Lord Jesus

Christ, come to Zion at the end of the 70th Week of Daniel.

This is when He victoriously appears with the 144 Thousand (Revelation 14:1), who are also identified by Obadiah:
"And saviors [deliverers] shall come up on Mount Zion to judge the mount of Esau; and the kingdom shall be the Lords." (Obadiah 21; Revelation 11:15)

These obedient servants of God will *"follow the Lamb wherever He goes" (Revelation14: 4)* both physically and spiritually. They as the merciful saviors/deliverers will in fact be the compassionate instruments of the one and only compassionate Savior, the Lamb, the Lord Jesus Christ, unto Jew and Gentile alike, during the Day of the Lord's wrath.

These Day of the Lord soldiers of the Lamb are also indicated to be *"with Him"* at the battle of Armageddon:
*"These [the ten horns/kings] shall make war with the Lamb, and the Lamb shall overcome them: for He is Lord of lords, and King of kings: and they that are **with Him** are called, and chosen, and faithful." (Revelation 17:14)*

The 144 Thousand, as the earthly members of *"His army" (Revelation 19:19)* along with *"the armies which were in heaven" (Revelation 19:14)* indicating the angelic host of heaven (Daniel 4:35), will defeat *"the kings of the earth, and their armies" (Revelation 19:19)* when the Lord Jesus Christ comes as *"KING OF KINGS, AND LORD OF LORDS" (Revelation19: 16.*

He will also defeat *"the beast...and...the false prophet...These both were cast alive into a lake of fire burning with brimstone. And the remnant [rest] were slain with the sword of Him that sat upon the horse which sword proceeded out of His mouth."*
(Revelation 19:20, 21)

These events describe, in brief, the final and culminating battle of the great and dreadful Day of the Lord, *"the battle of that great day of God Almighty' (Revelation 16:14)*, which is the renowned battle of Armageddon.

After the Day of the Lord judgment ends at Armageddon, the 144 Thousand will continue to *"follow Him wherever He goes" (Revelation 14:4)* becoming a part of that great gathering of God's people (Genesis 49:10; Psalm 102:21, 22; Hosea 1:11, 3:5; Micah 5:4) who enter and populate the promised land during the literal 1,000 year earthly rule of Christ called the Millennium (Revelation 20:1-6).

The 144 Thousand - Their Source
The 12 Tribes of Israel

The twelve tribes of Israel as a group are listed in Genesis 49:1-28 when the dying patriarch Jacob prophesies to his twelve sons:
*"And Jacob called unto his sons, and said, Gather yourselves together, that I may tell you that which shall befall you **<u>in the last days</u>**." (Genesis 49:1)*

The significance of this list of the twelve sons of Jacob is that it appears to provide the basic structure for the list of the twelve tribes found in Revelation 7:4-8. The tribes are listed in Revelation 7:3-8, the last time in Scripture, when the 144 Thousand are sealed for protection (Revelation 9:4) for their future Day of the Lord ministry.

Although there are changes in the order and the specific sons listed, the list in Revelation 7:4-8 has within it definite identifying features showing that this prophesy of Jacob found in the Genesis 49 list has the same underlying structure as the list in Revelation 7:4-8. The sons of Leah are first, then the sons of the two handmaids who are followed by the sons of Rachel, which is the general outline for both lists.

In verse one of Genesis 49 Jacob indicates that what he is going to say will have its effect *"in the last days"* which points to the time of the end as the period when these prophesies will take place. This prophetic section of the Word of God provides definite insight for those who will be sealed during Daniel's 70th Week, the last remaining week of the seventy weeks which were determined upon Daniel's people and their holy city Jerusalem:
"Seventy weeks are determined upon thy people and upon thy holy city." (Daniel 9:24)

*"And Jacob called unto his sons, and said, Gather yourselves together, that I may tell you that which shall befall you **<u>in the last days</u>**. Gather yourselves together, and hear, ye sons of Jacob, and hearken unto Israel your father." (Genesis 49:1, 2)*

Then Jacob addresses his firstborn son Reuben:

"Reuben, thou art my firstborn, my might and the beginning of my strength, the excellency of dignity, and the excellency of power Unstable as water, thou shalt not excel, because thou went up to thy father's bed; then defiled thou it: he went up to my couch."
(Genesis 49:3, 4)

Jacob is referring to the sex sin Reuben committed with Bilhah, Rachel's handmaid, with whom Jacob fathered two sons, Dan and Naphtali. Reuben's heinous sin cancelled his birthright, showing his instability, not having the ability to excel due to this defiling conduct which also removed the possibility of God's blessing.

Simeon and Levi, who are the next two sons born of Leah to Jacob were involved in the cruel sin of mass murder when they slaughtered the defenseless people in the town of Shechem (Genesis 34). They also do not receive a blessing, instead Jacob pronounces a curse upon them:

"Simeon and Levi are brethren; instruments of cruelty are in their habitations. O my soul come not thou into their secret; unto their assembly, mine honor, be not thou united: for in their anger they slew a man, and in their self will they digged down a wall. Cursed be their anger, for it was fierce, and their wrath, for it was cruel. I will divide them in Jacob, and scatter them in Israel." (Genesis 49:7-9)

The most significant section of Jacob's prophecy comes in (v.8-12) when he speaks to his fourth son Judah:

"Judah, thou art he whom thy brethren shall praise: thy hand shall be in the neck of thine enemies, thy father's children shall bow down before thee. Judah is a lion's whelp, from the prey, my son, thou art gone up, he stooped down, he couched as a lion, and as an old lion, who shall rouse him up? The scepter shall not depart from Judah, not a lawgiver from between his feet, until Shiloh come, and unto Him shall the gathering of the people be. Binding his foal unto the vine, and his ass's colt unto the choice vine; he washed his garments in wine, and his clothes in the blood of grapes: His eyes shall be red with wine, and his teeth white with milk." (Genesis 49:8-12)

The first two verses indicate the supremacy of Judah over his eleven brothers, his future military prowess and the position Judah would and will take in the order of the twelve tribes of Israel, for out of the loins of Judah kings would come forth (Genesis 49:10).

The focus here is upon the King of kings and Lord of lords the Savior of mankind, the Son of God and Jewish Messiah, the Lord Jesus Christ, God Incarnate, for the Lord Jesus Christ descended from the tribe of Judah (Hebrews 7:14). This is the reason Judah is first in the order of the last days tribal list in Revelation 7:4-8.

Judah, being placed in the first position of the sons of Jacob, began in the book of Numbers where he is listed as the first of the standard bearers *"toward the rising of the sun" (Numbers 2:3)*. Judah is the first tribe to give an offering (Numbers 7:12) and the first place went the standard of the camp of Judah according to their armies.

The Lord Jesus Christ is called *"Shiloh"* in Genesis 49:10 meaning *"The Peaceful Ruler"* showing the promise of the Ruler Who would come *"in the last days"* when *"unto Him shall the gathering of the people be"*. This refers to that future time when the twelve tribes will gather to Him, which is fulfilled in Revelation 14:1 when the 144 Thousand are seen with *"the Lamb"* on *"mount Zion" (Revelation 14:1)*.

The 144 Thousand will gather unto the Lord Jesus along with those Israelites who will be redeemed at the end of the 70th Week of Daniel (Isaiah 59:20; Romans 11:25, 26). *"The woman"* of Revelation 12, who represents the 70th Week faithful of Israel, will also be present at this great gathering of God's earthly people as indicated by the prophet Micah:
"Therefore will He [Messiah] give them [Israel] up until the time [End of the 70th Week/End of The Time of Jacob's Trouble] that she [Israel] which travails has brought forth [all Israel saved]: then the remnant [remainder/rest] of His brethren [the woman/faithful of Israel] shall return unto the children [sons] of Israel [the 144 Thousand]." (Micah 5:3)

These three distinct groups of Jews will gather unto their Messiah (Genesis 49:10; Psalm 102:21, 22; Hosea 1:11, 3:5), the Lord Jesus Christ, at the end of the 70th Week of Daniel. They will populate the land of Israel during the Millennium (Revelation 20:1-6) when the

Lord Jesus will physically rule on earth with a *"rod of iron" (Psalm 2:9; Revelation 19:15) "upon the throne of His father David" (Isaiah 9:7; Luke 1:32).*

Zebulun, the tenth son born to Jacob, is listed next in order that all the sons of Leah, Jacob's lawful wife, would come first for she bore six of his sons: Reuben, Simeon, Levi, Judah, Issachar and Zebulun. Jacob, who is now on his deathbed, shows his recognition of God's sovereign plan in selecting the Godly Leah who gave him half of his twelve sons. She also was buried in the cave of Machpelah with Jacob, in the family burial place where the patriarchs Abraham, Isaac and their wives were laid to rest (Genesis 49:31).

Zebulun's blessing would come through him being *"a haven of ships"* as *"his border shall be unto Zidon"* which is located on the northern coasts of the Promised Land on the Mediterranean Sea.

Issachar, is the last of Leah's sons:
"Issachar is a strong ass couching down between two burdens: And he saw that rest was good, and the land that it was pleasant; and bowed his shoulder to bear, and became a servant unto tribute." (Genesis 49:14, 15)

Issachar is a bearer of burdens who acknowledged the value of rest and the pleasantness of the promised land in that future day which is now taking place as prophesied here. It is evident that Israel has been transformed from a literal desert to a fruitful and productive land during the last sixty years [1948-2008] following the Jews return to their homeland.

After the sons of Leah are complete, Jacob speaks to his son Dan:
"Dan shall judge his people, as one of the tribes of Israel. Dan shall be a serpent by the way, an adder in the path, that bites the horse heels, so that his rider shall fall backward. I have waited for Thy salvation O Lord." (Genesis 49:16-18)

Dan, whose name literally means "He judged", is the firstborn of Bilhah, Rachel's handmaid. Although Dan is not one of the tribes sealed in the end times list of Revelation 7:4-8 he will be present then to perform the act of judging his people. This may include pleading their cause or contending for his brethren as this word *"Shall judge"* also means: To avenge, plead the cause, or contend.

Dan's serpent-like description vividly illustrates the characteristics of a small subtle entity having the physical ability to bring down the high and mighty warrior mounted upon a horse alluding to the likely defeat of a military foe.

These actions along with contending for his brethren during the last days fits with prophecies of wars being frequent in the land of Israel during that time (Joel 2; Ezekiel 38, 39). Dan will wait for the Lord to provide salvation/deliverance from these, his enemies, in that day.

The next son of Jacob is Gad, Leah's handmaid Zilpah's firstborn:
"Gad, a troop shall overcome him: but he shall overcome at the last." (Genesis 49:19)
He replaces Levi in the tribal lists found in the book of Numbers for Levi, the priestly tribe, is God's portion and was no longer included in the majority of the lists of the sons of Jacob.

Gad's future in the last days is also framed with a military tone as he is overcome at the first by a troop. However, in the end he is victorious, which could point to the possibility of an early defeat at the hands of the Antichrist when he initially invades the land after the mid-point of the 70th Week of Daniel when he:
"Shall devour the whole earth, and shall tread it down, and break it in pieces…when the Assyrian shall come into our land: and when he shall tread in our palaces" (Daniel 7:23; Micah 5:5a).

This crusade of the Antichrist is further described:
"And his power shall be mighty, but not by his own power: and he shall destroy wonderfully, and shall prosper, and practice, and shall destroy the mighty and the holy people [Israelites]." (Daniel 8:24)

"And he shall enter also into the glorious land [Israel]…And he shall plant the tabernacles of his palace between the seas in the glorious holy mountain [Mount Zion]." (Daniel 11:41, 45)
In the end, Gad and his brethren of the other tribes of Israel will come forth as gold when they go to battle along *"with the Lamb"*

(Revelation 17:14) the Lord Jesus Christ at *"the battle of that great day of God" (Revelation 16:14)* the battle of Armageddon which is described in Revelation 19:11-21.

"Out of Asher his bread shall be fat, and he shall yield royal dainties." (Genesis 49:20)

Asher, who is the last son born of Zilpah, will receive the blessings of richness by experiencing bountiful plenty during the latter days in the Promised Land. So rich in fact that it is here described as delicacies of royal quality. This supply of food will likely be brought forth and shared with all of the other tribes by the people of the tribe of Asher whose name literally means "happy".

"Naphtali is a hind let loose: he gives goodly words." (Genesis 49:20)

The last son born of Bilhah is described as a female deer that is set free or sent forth. This newfound liberty of Naphtali produces good and pleasant speech or communication during the last days. The tribe of Naphtali occupied the land of southern Galilee where the Lord Jesus ministered and spoke most of His parables and performed the majority of His miracles.

"Joseph is a fruitful bough, even a fruitful bough by a well; whose branches run over the wall: The archers have sorely grieved him, and shot at him, and hated him: But his bow abode in strength, and the arms of his hands were made strong by the hands of the mighty God of Jacob; (from thence is the Shepherd, the Stone of Israel:) Even by the God of thy father, who shall help thee; and by the Almighty, Who shall bless thee with blessings of heaven above, blessings of the deep that lie under, blessings of the breasts, and of the womb: The blessings of thy father have prevailed above the blessings of my progenitors unto the utmost bound of the everlasting hills: they shall be on the head of Joseph, and on the crown of the head of him that was separate from his brethren." (Genesis 49:22-26)

Joseph, Rachel's firstborn, receives the longest and most extensive blessing from the lips of his father Jacob. Although the royal tribe of Judah has the Messianic pre-eminence, Joseph's rich blessing reveals Jacob's great love for his firstborn son of Rachel, Leah's younger sister.

He bestows upon him the blessing of overflowing fruitfulness having overcome the afflictions of the archer's bow and the separation from his brethren. Jacob details Joseph's present (v.22) his past (v.23, 24) and his future blessings (v.25, 26) laying full emphasis upon the help and supernatural power of God Almighty.

He utilizes the following five titles for God emphasizing exactly Who will be responsible for these miraculous future blessings which Jacob pronounced upon his eleventh son Joseph:
1. The Mighty God of Jacob (v.24)
2. The Shepherd (v.24)
3. The Stone [Rock] of Israel (v.24)
4. The God of thy father (v.25)
5. The Almighty (v.25)

Joseph will of a certainty receive the bountiful blessings of heaven, the unfathomable blessings of the deep, and the fruitful multiplication of his tribe through the matriarchal blessings of breast and womb. Jacob summarizes this magnificent bounty of God's goodness in (v.26) by revealing that his blessing will prevail even above the blessings of Abraham and Isaac the patriarchs who came before him. These blessings bestowed upon Joseph and his last days descendants will reach unto the farthest known boundary of the everlasting hills.

The tribes of Ephraim and Manasseh are represented under the name of their father Joseph as Manasseh's name appears in the Revelation 7:4-8 list and Ephraim's descendants are those sealed under the name of Joseph for Ephraim and Manasseh were Joseph's only sons.

"Benjamin shall ravin as a wolf: in the morning he shall devour the prey, and at night he shall divide the spoil." (Genesis 49:27)
The last, the least, and the littlest, is the much-loved tribe of Benjamin whose name means *"son of my old age"*. He was specifically given this name by his father Jacob (Genesis 35:18). He is the twelfth son of Jacob and the last son born of Rachel who died during his birth.

Benjamin is described as eating voraciously like a wolf in the wild when it devours and consumes its prey. This brings to mind the picture of the might and strength of a warrior who has the power to fully overcome the enemy in the heat of battle who later divides the spoils of his overwhelming victory among his fellow soldiers.

Matthew Henry, commenting on this verse, said that the tribe of Benjamin shall be "Warlike, strong and daring, enriching themselves with the spoils of their enemies." Some notable Bible characters from the tribe of Benjamin are:
1. King Saul
2. Jonathan, son of Saul
3. Mordecai
4. Esther
5. Saul of Tarsus/Apostle Paul

The common characteristics this group manifests in Scripture portray a clear picture of those future Benjamites clearly prophesied by Jacob and pointed out by Matthew Henry. This small but significant tribe will continue to display these most descriptive warlike attributes during *"the last days"* as foretold by Jacob.

Then, there shall be *"wars and rumors of wars" (Matthew 24:6)* during which time the twelve tribes including this last little tribe of Benjamin will take a most significant and victorious role.

While Jacob's first three sons, Reuben, Simeon and Levi receive a negative prophecy, of the remaining nine, five will have success against their foes:
1. Judah's hand shall be in the neck of his enemies. (v. 8)
2. Dan shall be a serpent that causes the rider to fall. (v. 17)
3. Gad shall overcome a troop. (v. 19)
4. Joseph's bow abode in strength. (v. 24)
5. Benjamin shall devour his prey and divide the spoil. (v. 27)

This military might has been evident down through Israel's history and will continue to be prevalent during the time of the end when the twelve tribes will band together once again to defeat their enemies under the leadership of their Messiah, the Lord Jesus Christ (Micah 5:4-8; Revelation 17:14, 19:11-21). Since the 144 Thousand will definitely come from *"the twelve tribes of Israel' (Revelation 7:3-8)* it is necessary to briefly review the history of these tribes.

When Jacob took his family down into Egypt they numbered *"threescore and ten" (Genesis 46:27)*, but when Moses brought Jacob's family out of Egypt a little over four centuries later it is estimated that they had grown to over 1.5 million. After 40 years of wilderness wandering the division of the land by Joshua took place and the tribes took up permanent residence in the land of Canaan living together as a unit until the kingdom was divided after the death of King Solomon.

These ten tribes made up the northern kingdom:
(1) Reuben, (2) Simeon, (3) Issachar, (4) Zebulon, (5) Dan, (6) Gad, (7) Asher, (8) Naphtali, (9) Manasseh, (10) Ephraim

Judah and Benjamin are the two tribes of the southern kingdom. They controlled Jerusalem where the tribe of Levi continued to serve the Lord in the temple built by Solomon although many Levites also lived among the ten tribes of the northern kingdom.

In 722 B.C. the ten northern tribes were defeated and taken into captivity and dispersed abroad by Sennacherib the Assyrian king. He made an attempt to do the same to the two southern tribes but was unsuccessful due to the miraculous intervention of God
(II Kings 19:15-37).

In 586 B.C. the two southern tribes, Judah and Benjamin, along with the remaining Levites, were defeated by Nebuchadnezzar who destroyed the city of Jerusalem and Solomon's temple. The two southern tribes were taken captive and moved to Babylon. After 70 years approximately 50,000, a small minority of the Babylonian captives from the tribes of Judah, Benjamin and Levi returned to the land of Israel to rebuild the temple (Ezra 1:5, 2:2) under Zerubbabel's leadership.

Approximately 80 years later Ezra the priest/scribe returned to Jerusalem from Babylon to bring revival to those already in the land of Israel (Ezra 7-10). The Levites, Nethinims [temple servants] and people of Israel from the tribes of Judah and Benjamin who came with Ezra totaled approximately 1800.

Then, Nehemiah returned to the Promised Land from Babylon

about 14 years after Ezra and rebuilt the wall around the city of Jerusalem (Nehemiah 1-6) along with members of the tribes of Levi, Judah, and Benjamin who were already in the land.

While there were only three tribes involved in these returns from Babylon, after the temple and wall were rebuilt and Jerusalem was once again inhabited, many Jews from the other tribes made the pilgrimage to their holy city. This is evidenced by the gathering recorded four centuries later on the day of Pentecost in A.D.33:

*"And there were dwelling at Jerusalem, Jews, devout men, out of **every nation** under heaven. And they were all amazed and marveled, saying one to another, Behold are not all these which speak Galileans? And how hear we every man in our own tongue, wherein we were born? Parthians, and Medes, and Elamites, and the dwellers in Mesopotamia, and in Judea, and Cappodocia, in Pontus, and Asia, Phrygia, and Pamphylia, in Egypt, and in the parts of Libya about Cyrene, and strangers of Rome, Jews and proselytes, Cretes and Arabians, we do hear them speak in our tongues the wonderful works of God." (Acts 2:5, 7-10)*

This multi-national gathering of Jews from all parts of the Roman Empire likely has in its makeup members from the northern ten tribes for these Jews came from as far as the city of Rome. This passage reveals that in the centuries since their dispersion the Jews had migrated to the farthest reaches of the Roman Empire.

While the ten tribes are called "The ten lost tribes" by some in the present day indicating that it is not known where or whether they still exist, they are definitely not lost in the eyes and heart of Almighty God.

About 40 years after this day of Pentecost, in 70 A.D., the Roman armies of Titus completely destroyed Jerusalem and the rebuilt temple which was prophesied by the Lord Jesus Christ (Matthew 24:2). Most of the Israelites were either killed or scattered at that time although there was an uprising of some Jews in the land called the Bar-Kochba rebellion a little over six decades later [A.D.130-135].

This last attempt by the Jews to free themselves was summarily and brutally crushed by the army of the Roman emperor Hadrian.

During the centuries that have passed since this final purge of the Jews the Promised Land has been controlled by various kings and rulers.

The Lord in His preparation for the end times has brought His earthly people back into the holy land once again and they now occupy their holy city Jerusalem which are definite pre-requisites for the 70th Week of Daniel (Daniel 9:24).

The twelve tribes listed in Revelation 7:4-8 may already be represented in the land of Israel. But, the great number [144 Thousand] of young men that will be sealed in that future day indicates the likely possibility that many of these young men will still be scattered throughout the earth.

They definitely will all be in the land at the end of the 70th Week of Daniel (Revelation 14:1) when they appear in Jerusalem with the Lord on Mt. Zion. However, it is not necessary for them to be in the land of Israel when they are sealed just prior to the beginning of the Day of the Lord.

Until recently the United States of America was the home of the largest Jewish population. Now [2008], the land of Israel (Approx. 7 Million) is the largest with the U.S.A. (Approx. 6 Million) in second place and Europe (Approx. 1.5 Million) in third.

The region formerly called the U.S.S.R., although rapidly dwindling in Jewish population due to the Jews return to the land of Israel, still has approximately 435 Thousand professing Jews making it the fourth largest area.

The focus of evangelism for the church in these last days must be centered upon the Jew with emphasis upon these areas of the world where the majority of the twelve tribes of Israel now reside.

Even though Paul was unmercifully persecuted and soundly rejected by the great majority of the Jews during his ministry, he continued to go to their synagogues in each city attempting to win them to Christ as revealed in these texts (Acts 9:20, 13:5, 14:1, 17:1, 10, 17, 18:4, 19).

He was simply following his heart (Romans 1:15, 16, 10:1) and the method that His Lord used during His ministry. For, at the end of the Lord Jesus Christ's First Coming, He gave this brief description of His public ministry:

"I spoke openly to the world; I ever taught in the synagogue, and in the temple, whither the Jews always resort; and in secret have I said nothing." (John 18:20)

In God's purpose there is coming a day, during the 70th Week of Daniel, when *"the veil shall be taken away" (II Corinthians 3:16b)* from the spiritual eyes of His earthly people the Jews. Then, their *"Redeemer shall come to Zion, and unto them that turn from transgression in Jacob, saith the Lord." (Isaiah 59:20)*

"And so all Israel shall be saved: as it is written, There shall come out of Zion the Deliverer, and shall turn away ungodliness from Jacob." (Romans 11:26)

But at the present hour *"the veil is upon their heart" (II Corinthians 3:15)* and the age old methods used by the Lord Jesus Christ and the Apostle Paul are still the best ways to reach the Jews. They utilized Old Testament Messianic preaching (Luke 4:15-21; Acts 13:16-39, 17:1-3, 18:28) and Holy Spirit-led confrontational one on one evangelism (John 3:1-21, 4:1-26; Acts 16:31, 18:4, 19:8).

In the purpose of God, it is the duty of the Church of Jesus Christ to pray for the Lord to send forth laborers into His harvest. They must focus their Holy Spirit filled soul-winning expertise upon the earthly people of God, the Jews, wherever they may be found as we close in on the Second Coming of the Lord Jesus Christ.

The time is drawing near when these young men (Psalm 110:3), the 144 Thousand, will be called, prepared and later sealed for their Day of the Lord service to God. This great conversion of the earthly people of God may well take place during the powerful restoration ministry of the Elijah-like prophet whom God will send to His people.

He will of necessity follow the pattern of his two predecessors, Elijah and John the Baptist, by preaching repentance and revival, *"Turning hearts…Restoring all things" (Malachi 4:5, 6;*

Matthew 17:11) in the process.

It is likely that the Lord will use this mighty prophet to bring revival to the Church of Jesus Christ and spearhead the mass evangelization of His earthly people, the Jews, including the 144 Thousand. The 144 Thousand are given a unique title that points to this very possibility:
*"These were redeemed from among men, being the **first-fruits unto God and to the Lamb**." (Revelation 14:4c)*

These young men will be the first Jews to be redeemed during the 70th Week of Daniel, which is the last week of the *"Seventy weeks are determined upon thy people and thy holy city" (Daniel 9:24)*.

There will be many Jews redeemed later during this restored *"holy covenant" (Daniel 11:28-32)* Jewish dispensation when God will surely bring to pass His great and precious promises to His earthly people (Isaiah 59:20; Zechariah 13:8, 9; Romans 11:25, 26) the Jews.

The 144 Thousand
Their Supernatural Calling

The spiritual condition of these young Hebrew men at the time of their sealing (Revelation 7:3-8) with the name of God and the Lamb (Revelation 14:1) is established by the Biblical record based upon the following truths:
1. Their descriptive title: *"The servants [bond-slaves] of our God" (Revelation 7:3)* **before** they are sealed
2. Three Bible examples of other redeemed men marked by God
    a. Old Testament example: (Ezekiel 9:4-7)
    b. New Testament example #1: (Revelation 3:12)
    c. New Testament example #2: (Revelation 22:4)
3. The Lord would never place His holy name (Revelation 7:3, 14:1) upon unredeemed men.

These truths establish the fact of their redemption prior to their sealing. Therefore, it is necessary to consider the impact that their redemption and subsequent preparation has upon the Church of Jesus Christ for the Church will be the source or seedbed for many of these young Jewish disciples of the Lord Jesus Christ (Revelation 14:4).

The Church must now focus its evangelistic efforts upon *"the Jew first"* as was the priority of the Lord Jesus Christ and the Apostle Paul (Matthew 15:24; Romans 1:15, 16) for these 144 Thousand young Jewish servants of God must be redeemed and prepared for their end times Redemption Ministry.

It is possible that many present-day Jews are unaware of their lineage as demonstrated by the following brief but illustrative true account:
Two brothers were recently made aware of their real estate ownership in Austria. A multi-million dollar structure belonged to their family prior to World War II and was seized by the Nazis in the late 1930's. A recent investigation of the rightful ownership took place and they were told of their good fortune.

Through the unfolding of these events they found out that their mother, now deceased, who had brought them to the U.S.A. before full-scale war had broken out, was a Jewess and kept her background secret when they fled the Nazis and found refuge in the U.S.A.

It was not until they, the two brothers, as the surviving property owners, were sought out that they were made aware of their Jewish lineage which had been lost and unknown to them in merely one generation. This scenario has likely been repeated down through the ages, as the Jews have been the targets of various purges and persecutions from the beginning of their existence.

This type of event would cause many others whose bloodline descends from the twelve sons of Jacob to be lost through the ages…lost, that is, to man, but definitely not lost in the eyes and heart of Almighty God.

Moses was a man who descended from the tribe of Levi, but was raised from an infant in the palace of the Pharaoh of Egypt. How long was it until he realized his lineage and God called him to deliver his people from bondage? He may have remained unaware of his bloodline well into adulthood.

Many generations have come and gone since 70 A.D. when the Jews were scattered after the destruction of the temple and the city of Jerusalem which destruction also eliminated any and all written ancestry records of the twelve tribes of Israel

The ascertaining of exactly who is a Jew and the tribe of Israel from whence they came can only be determined by Almighty God. Just as in the past Biblical record, the Lord will continue His practice of choosing out from among His people those whom He calls and prepares as His servants.

Like Moses, the servant of God (Exodus 14:31), the 144 Thousand may be initially unaware that their bloodline comes directly from one of the twelve sons of Israel who are listed in Revelation 7:3-8. However, when God calls, He will also make them aware of His plan for their lives in much the same manner that He has done with His servants of old that He has called, prepared and mightily used for His service down through the centuries.

The Lord definitely has spoken to His past servants through supernatural communication:
1. Abraham: (Genesis 12:1-3, 7, 13:14-17, 15:1-21, 17:1-22, 18:1-33, 21:12, 13, 22:1-18)
2. Isaac: (Genesis 26:24, 25)
3. Jacob: (Genesis 28:10-22, 32:1, 2, 24-32, 35:1)
4. Moses: (Exodus 3:1-4:26)
5. Samuel: (I Samuel 3:1-21)
6. Isaiah: (Isaiah 6:1-13)
7. Jeremiah: (Jeremiah 1:1-19)
8. Ezekiel: (Ezekiel 1:1-28, 2:1-3:27)
9. Daniel: (Daniel 7:1-28, 8:1-27, 9:20-27, 10:1-12:13)
10. John the Baptist: (John 1:23-34)
11. Paul the Apostle: (Acts 9:3-16, 16:6-10)
12. John the Apostle: (Revelation 1:1, 10-20)

When these supernatural communications are surveyed a number of common practices of God unfold:
1. He gives promises and blessings to His servants.
2. He foretells the ministry of His servants.
3. He gives explicit personal details to His servants.

Three economies are covered in this list of God's servants, promise, law and grace with John the Baptist the transitional prophet (Matthew 11:13) between law and grace who knew exactly who he was (Isaiah 40:3; John 1:23) and specifically what he came to accomplish (John 1:23-34).

These future servants of God, the 144 Thousand, are entitled: *"the first-fruits unto God and to the Lamb" (Revelation 14:4)* indicating that they are the first Jews to be redeemed during the restored *"holy covenant" (Daniel 11:28-32)* period, which is the 70th Week of Daniel.

They are the first of a great company of Jews who will follow (Isaiah 59:20; Romans 11:25, 26) when they are redeemed at the end of those seven years when the Lord will *"bring in everlasting righteousness" (Daniel 9:24)*.

This period of time has been called by some "The last Jewish dispensation" when God will once again deal with His earthly people, the Jews by reverting to the Old Covenant. This Old Covenant period will bring with it similar circumstances and practices that were prevalent during the first 483 years of this 490 year period as evidenced by the following Old and New Testament prophetic texts:

1. The Jews will be a "*people*"/nation (Daniel 9:24)
2. The Jews will be in their Promised Land
    (Deuteronomy 30:5-9; Daniel 9:24; Matthew 24:16)
3. The Jews will occupy their "*holy city*" Jerusalem
    (Daniel 9:24)
4. The Lord will send "*Elijah*" to revive/restore (Malachi 4:5, 6; Matthew 17:11; Mark 9:12)
5. "*The holy covenant*" will be restored (Daniel 11:28-32)
6. "*The temple of God*" will be rebuilt
    (Daniel 11:31; II Thessalonians 2:1- 4; Revelation 11:1, 2)
7. "*The holy place*" included (Matthew 24:15)
8. "*The regular sacrifices*" will be instituted
    (Daniel 8:11, 12, 9:27, 11:31, 12:11)
9. The Jews will "*worship*" in "*the temple of God*"
    (Revelation 11:1.2)
10. "*The Sabbath*" will be reinstated (Matthew 24:20)
11. The Lord will send His "*prophet[s]*" to His people
    (Malachi 4:5, 6; Revelation 11:3-17)
12. "*The tribes of Israel*" will be recognized (Revelation 7:3-8)

During this last seven year period, the 70th Week of Daniel, the 144 Thousand will be redeemed, called, trained and serve the Lord. They too will receive supernatural communication from the Lord just as His servants of old who were told of their calling and future ministry as faithful *"servants of our God" (Revelation 7:3)*. They will provide their vital Redemption Ministry as the end of the age kingdom of priests unto those whom God will call.

The 144 Thousand
The Passing of the Torch - [Part I]

From the beginning of Biblical history God has always prepared the next generation to represent Him and His Word on earth before the proceeding generation passed on into eternity. Moses trained Joshua and Paul trained Timothy and the Lord trained His disciples before they "Passed the Torch" to the next generation. This illustrates just a few instances of God's practice of working in the lives of successive generations of His servants.

So it will be at the end of the age when the saints are removed from the earth by rapture. God will prepare the next generation to carry His Word to those who will be redeemed during the Day of the Lord. Then, He will judge Jew and Gentile alike, and in the process purge the nation of Israel so that at the end of the 70th Week of Daniel *"all Israel shall be saved" (Romans 11:25, 26).*

Revelation chapter seven is the key section of Scripture showing "The Passing of the Torch" as the saints are raptured bringing an innumerable multitude to heaven (Revelation 7:9-17) after the 144 Thousand are sealed (Revelation 7:1-8) for protection (Revelation 9:4) during their coming Day of the Lord ministry.

The saints will be "<u>Raptured from Wrath</u>", rescued from the persecution of the Antichrist just before the Lord brings His wrath upon those that remain on the earth, exactly as He promised,
(I Thessalonians 1:10, 5:1-10) but, He will not leave the earth without a human witness.

This great company of Jews, the 144 Thousand, will *"follow the Lamb wherever He goes" (Revelation 14:4)* indicating their full surrender and total commitment to the Lord Jesus Christ. They will be model disciples, witnessing of the Lord's redemption to those that do not know Him during those days of devastating fiery judgment of the Day of the Lord's wrath.

How will this great company of the sons of Israel be chosen? Will they be saved before or after the rapture of the saints? Are they merely physical descendants of the twelve tribes of Israel who are sealed, or are they already believing sons of God before the sealing takes place?

If the Lord continues to operate the way He has throughout the ages, these who are sealed will already be mightily prepared *"servants of our God" (Revelation 7:3)* whom He has chosen and who will already have fully surrendered their lives to the service of the Lamb their King. The Scripture clearly indicates that they are:
"Sealed...servants of God...children (sons) of Israel...having His (the Lamb's) Father's name written in their foreheads...could learn that song...were redeemed from the earth...not defiled with women for they are virgins...follow the Lamb wherever He goes...were redeemed from among men, being the first-fruits unto God and the Lamb...in their mouth was found no guile: for they are without fault before the Throne of God." (Revelation 7:3-8, 14:1-5)

This impeccable group of God's faithful servants are duly called and qualified to be the Lord's faithful representatives during the most trying of circumstances ever experienced by a child of God. They are a choice group of God's bond-servants indeed, who fully know their position and calling and willingly give themselves to their precious Lord for His service whatever it might be.

These are not just a generic group of Jews mystically selected to be protected during the Day of the Lord in order that the physical seed of Israel survives the judgment of God. No, this is a prime group of men, chosen saints of God who have been called out of the twelve tribes for *"such a time as this" (Esther 4:14.)* The Lord will bring upon all of mankind His fiery judgment of planet earth and its inhabitants which is called *"the great and dreadful Day of the Lord" (Malachi 4:5)* also described as the wrath of God (Isaiah 13:6-10; Zephaniah 1:14, 15).

This group, because of the complete description given them in Revelation 7:3-8, 14:1-5, is clearly identified as first of all *"sealed'*. This indicates the protection of God **in the midst of** (Revelation 9:4) His Day of the Lord wrath. The Lord in the past has removed His own people prior to His judgment as shown during the worldwide cataclysmic flood when He rescued the family of Noah in the ark.

He also *"delivered just Lot"* and his family before the fiery judgment fell upon Sodom and Gomorrah. But, in this instance, the Lord gives the 144 Thousand His name (Revelation 7:3, 14:1) upon their foreheads to protect them **in the midst of** His judgment.

In Ezekiel chapter nine a number of parallels are recorded which are similar to what is going to happen just prior to the Day of the Lord's wrath as described in Revelation chapter seven. First of all it must be emphasized that it is the Lord, the sovereign Ruler of the universe, the God of heaven and earth, Who is bringing this wrath upon the earth and its inhabitants. The end of Revelation chapter six confirms this to be the case:
"For the great day of His wrath is come; and who shall be able to stand?" (Revelation 6:17)

This statement supplies us with the fact of Who is responsible for the impending judgment which will begin when the first trumpet is blown in chapter eight. Ezekiel chapter eight also verifies that the Lord is responsible for what occurs in chapter nine:
"He cried also in mine ears with a loud voice, saying, Cause them that have charge over the city to draw near, even every man with his destroying weapon in his hand. And, behold six men came from the way of the higher gate, which lies toward the north, and every man a slaughter weapon in his hand; and one man among them was clothed with linen, with a writer's inkhorn by his side: and they went in, and stood by the brazen altar. And the glory of God was gone up from the cherub, whereupon he was, to the threshold of the house of God. And He called to the man clothed with linen, which had the writer's inkhorn by his side; And the Lord said unto him, Go through the midst of the city, through the midst of Jerusalem, and set a mark (signature) upon the foreheads of the men that sigh and that cry for all the abominations that be done in the midst thereof. And to the others he said in mine hearing, Go ye after him through the city, and smite: let not your eye spare, neither have ye pity: Slay utterly old and young both maids, and little children: but come not near any man upon whom is the mark (signature); and begin at My sanctuary."
(Ezekiel 9:1-6)

Here, in Ezekiel's vision, the Lord commands His representatives to bring His judgment upon the inhabitants of Jerusalem. But, before the judgment falls, He supernaturally protects His own and sets His mark or signature upon their foreheads. **In the midst of** His judgment He protects His own.

In the book of the Revelation a similar event occurs:
"And after these things I saw four angels standing on the four corners of the earth, holding the four winds of the earth, that the wind should not blow on the earth, nor on the sea, not on any tree. And I saw another angel ascending from the east, having the seal of the living God: and he cried with a loud voice to the four angels, to whom it was given to hurt the earth and the sea, Saying hurt not the earth, neither the sea, nor the trees, till we have sealed the servants of our God in their foreheads. And I heard the number of them which were sealed: and there were sealed and hundred and forty and four thousand of all the tribes of the children (sons) of Israel."
(Revelation 7:1-4)

God sends His representatives to place His protective signature or mark upon those He is going to protect. In Revelation 7:3, *"the seal of the living God"* applied by His angel is later identified as *"His...name written in their foreheads" (Revelation 14:1).*

In Ezekiel the word for *"mark"* could also be translated *"signature"* and therefore is very similar with what will take place in Revelation chapter seven just prior to God's judgment, the Day of the Lord's wrath. Here again, the Lord supernaturally protects His own **in the midst of** His Day of the Lord judgment. Another parallel is recorded in Ezekiel 9:3:
"And the glory of the God of Israel was gone up from the cherub, whereupon he was, to the threshold of the house."

This action taken by God before the protection of His own and the judgment of those in Jerusalem is illustrated by the promise of the Lord to the saints found in I Thessalonians 4:17:
"Then we which are alive and remain shall be caught up together with them in the clouds to meet the Lord in the air: and so shall we ever be with the Lord."

The rapture of the saints, the blessed hope and glorious appearing of the great God and our Savior to take His own to heaven illustrates a similar event. It took place in the vision of Ezekiel as God removes His glory from its place, which is similar to the saints departing earth by rapture, when His glory, the saints (John 17:22) are then removed.

The timing of this great event is just before His wrath begins in Revelation 8:1. He promised the saints they would be delivered from the wrath to come (I Thessalonians 1:10, 5:1-10), and so He will rapture the saints just before it begins. Just before He seals the 144 Thousand with His signature, the saints will "Pass the Torch" to the 144 Thousand sons of Israel.

Five parallels or similarities to the Revelation account are seen in Ezekiel's vision:
1. The Lord is responsible for the judgment (Ezekiel 9:1-6 Revelation 6:17)
2. The Lord's representatives bring the judgment (Ezekiel 9:1-6; Revelation 8-11, 15-18)
3. The Lord's glory is removed before the judgment (Ezekiel 9:3; Revelation 7:9-17)
4. The Lord marks His own before the judgment (Ezekiel 9:4, 11; Revelation 7:1-8)
5. The Lord protects His own in the midst of judgment (Ezekiel 9:4-6; Revelation 3:10, 7:1-8, 9:4)

In addition, there are two other groups who have the Lord's name written upon them. The over-comers of the church of Philadelphia (Revelation 3:12) and the *"servants"* of the Lamb in heaven (Revelation 22:3, 4).

Both of these groups are shown to be saints before they have the name of the Lord written upon them. These two groups of saints receive these blessings of eternal rewards for their overcoming lives and service to the Lord.

Right after the sealing of the 144 Thousand (Revelation 7:3-8), the raptured saints are seen in heaven:
"After this I beheld, and, lo, a great multitude, which no man could number, of all nations, and kindreds, and people, and tongues, stood

before the throne, and before the Lamb, clothed with white robes, and palms in their hands; And cried with a loud voice, saying, Salvation to our God which sits upon the throne, and unto the Lamb." (Revelation 7:9, 10)

This great multitude comes *"out of [the] great tribulation"* which indicates not the actual geographic location but the time period from whence they came. This just happens to be the right time period at this point in the chronology of the book of the Revelation for the saints to be raptured because we have come to the end of the Great Tribulation according to Revelation 6:12-17 and the Lord's parallel chronology in Matthew 24:29-31.

We are right on schedule as the Lord indicated:
*"Immediately **after** the tribulation of those days shall the sun be darkened, and the moon shall not give her light, and the stars shall fall from heaven, and the powers of the heavens shall be shaken." (Matthew 24:29)*

This is exactly where we are in the sequence of events in the book of the Revelation, for this is the sign which occurs **before** the Day of the Lord (Joel 2:30, 31), which is the wrath of God. It is about to occur with the removing of the seventh seal thereby opening the scroll which contains the wrath of God beginning with the first trumpet judgment.

The saints have been promised to be *"delivered from wrath"* (I Thessalonians 1:10, 5:9) by the God of heaven and the timing is perfectly exact. However, before we can move from Revelation 6 which ends with the sixth seal and the announcement of *"the great day of His wrath" (Revelation 6:17),* "The Passing of the Torch" must take place.

The 144 Thousand are sealed (Revelation 7:3-8) with the signature of God on their foreheads. Then the glory of God departs (Revelation 7:9ff). The saints are raptured just before the wrath of God begins. Then…1/2 hour of silence in heaven (Revelation 8:1)…all praise to the Lord of glory is silenced…for the first time in the history of heaven…all is quiet and still…the calm before the storm. The most prophesied event in Scripture, the Day of the Lord, is about to begin.

Then, the Lord initiates His fiery judgment of planet earth and its inhabitants with the progressive heavenly sequence of *"voices, and thunderings, and lightnings, and an earthquake"* followed by the sounding of the first trumpet (Revelation 8:1-7) all of which emanates from the Throne of God where all authority in heaven and earth dwells!

And so, "The Passing of the Torch" takes place. The saints are home in heaven (Revelation 7:9-17). The 144 Thousand are sealed, protected and ready to continue serving the Lord as His kingdom of priests during the coming Day of the Lord's Wrath when they will: *"follow the Lamb wherever He goes" (Revelation 14:4)* showing their complete dedication to His will and leading as they serve Him during those fiery and tumultuous days ahead.

The 144 Thousand
The Passing of the Torch - [Part II]

As we have seen in Part I, Revelation chapter seven focuses on two significant groups of God's children. The first is the 144 Thousand and the second is the great multitude in heaven, which are the resurrected and raptured saints of the ages. The 144 Thousand are now God's kingdom of priests on earth during the Day of the Lord's wrath and the resurrected and raptured saints are home in heaven.

If this chosen group of men, the 144 Thousand, are truly children of God, then why were they not raptured when the saints were caught up into heaven? How could they be God's children and not be raptured with the great multitude now in heaven? In order to answer these questions we must recognize just where we are in God's program.

At this point in time we are well into what is known as Daniel's 70th Week. The period known as the Day of the Lord is about to begin. God will be dealing with His chosen earthly people, the Jews, in these last seven years of Daniel's prophesied time period which is 490 years in duration (Daniel 9:24).

The 70th Week of Daniel is almost over, and, there may be but a few years left before these seven years are finished. We must recognize that the Lord always brings those whom He has chosen into His family the same way and that is *"by grace...through faith" (Ephesians 2:8)*.

In the Old Testament era that ran its course until John the Baptist, the Holy Spirit of God did not indwell all those who believed. This blessing of the indwelling Holy Spirit, was and now is *"the promise of the Father" (Luke 24:49; Acts 1:4, 2:33, 39)* which was given after Jesus ascended to heaven and was glorified on the day of Pentecost (Acts 2) as taught in the New Testament.

It is theoretically possible that the 144 Thousand will be redeemed under the Old Covenant that is in effect during these last seven years, which is the 70th Week of Daniel, and may not receive the indwelling Holy Spirit of God.

Then, when the rapture occurs, they will remain to serve the Lord as they do not have *"the earnest of the Spirit" (II Corinthians 1:22)* in their hearts. The earnest or down payment which is the indwelling Holy Spirit *"is the earnest of our inheritance until the redemption (rapture) of the purchased possession" (Ephesians 1:14)* which in short means that those with the indwelling Holy Spirit will be raptured and those without will not.

Those who believe God, just as Abraham: *"And he (Abraham) believed in the Lord, and He counted it to him for righteousness" (Genesis 15:6)*, will be bona-fide children of God. But, they might not possess the indwelling Spirit Who supplies the believer with the means whereby they are raptured into heaven.

The graves will open:
"The dead in Christ shall rise first, then we which are alive and remain (those with the indwelling Spirit) shall be caught up together with them in the clouds to meet the Lord in the air: and so shall we ever be with the Lord." (I Thessalonians 4:16, 17)

There are other believing Jews who will also remain on earth after the rapture. The *"two witnesses"* will prophesy for *"a thousand two hundred and three score days"* [3-1/2 years] (Revelation 11:3). The rapture occurs during this 3-1/2 year time period. *"The woman"* [faithful nation of Israel] too, will remain on earth during this same time period (Revelation 12:6)

During the 70th Week, God's plan of redemption may revert to the restored (Malachi 4:5, 6; Matthew 17:11) *"holy covenant"* [Old Covenant] *(Daniel 11:28-31)* as He once again deals with the nation of Israel just as He did during the previous 483 years or 69 weeks of Daniel's 70 weeks.

If that is the case, there will those believers in the Church who enter the 70th week of Daniel, but, when those last seven years begin (Daniel 9:24-27), God will once again deal with the Jew under the

Old Covenant.

And so, "The Passing of the Torch" will be accomplished. The Church saints will pass the torch to the 144 Thousand and they in turn will be the Lord's necessary kingdom of priests providing their Redemption Ministry during the Day of the Lord judgment.

This chosen group of men will remain on the earth as they *"follow the Lamb whithersoever He goes" (Revelation 14:4)* indicating their full and complete dedication to His will. This mighty group of disciples will witness of their redemption and their glorious Lord and Savior Jesus Christ to those who will remain, Jew and Gentile alike, during the great and dreadful Day of the Lord.

They will be supernaturally protected from the cataclysmic judgment of God as indicated in this text:
*"And it was commanded them that they should not hurt the grass of the earth, neither any green thing, neither any tree: but only those men which have **not** the seal (signature) of God in their foreheads." (Revelation 9:4)*

Here is the confirmation for the purpose of the signature of God in the foreheads of the 144 Thousand. These choice young men, the 144 Thousand, who have been supernaturally sealed at the beginning of the Day of the Lord's wrath, will be protected from the tormenting judgment of the fifth trumpet.

We must recognize that what has been written above is merely a **theory** of how things **may** unfold during the time of the end. However, it is based upon Biblical truth and could well be the way the Lord brings about His plan for the end times.

As the Scripture is examined God's plan for the 144 Thousand becomes clear for they have at least twelve descriptive attributes that provide the Bible student with the information necessary to determine their specific role during the Day of the Lord. The first of these twelve is found in Revelation 7:3:
"Hurt not the earth, neither the sea, nor the trees, till we have sealed the servants of our God in their foreheads."

We have already covered the sealing or signature of God in their foreheads, which provides their supernatural protection during the Day of the Lord. The second attribute tells of their duty to God. They are called *"servants"* which literally means "slave or bondservant". This title is reserved for those who have surrendered their lives to the Lord for His service and glory.

Paul, James, John, Peter, Moses and the prophets are some of the men that are described by this word in the New Testament. These are not just nominal or newly saved children of God, no, these are the "cream of the crop", the best there is on the planet, chosen and choice bond-servants of the Living God.

The third attribute mentioned is found in Revelation 7:4:
"And I heard the number of them which were sealed: and there were sealed and hundred and forty and four thousand of all the tribes of the children (sons) of Israel."

Here we learn that they are *"sons"* which is the meaning of this Greek word translated *"children"*, so, they are men. The Lord also makes it clear that their heritage or bloodline is from His earthly chosen people, the twelve tribes of the nation of Israel.

The tribe of Dan is omitted and the tribe of Ephraim, although missing in name, is sealed under Joseph as he had only two sons, Manasseh and Ephraim. This brings up another question, "Who is a Jew?" Is a Jew a self-proclaimed proselyte of Judaism? Is a Jew one who wears the orthodox garb and is seen on the news at the Wailing Wall? No, a Jew is one who is of the bloodline of the original twelve sons of Jacob as listed in Genesis 49.

Their fourth attribute is found in Revelation 14:1:
"And I looked, and, lo, a Lamb stood on the mount Zion, and with Him and hundred forty and four thousand."

These select servants of God are seen *"with the Lamb"*. It appears that they are inseparable as the Lord's presence on mount Zion at the end of the 70th week of Daniel is recorded. The next thing we are told concerns their ability:
"And no man could learn that song but the hundred and forty and

four thousand." (Revelation 14:3)

They will be the only men on earth that can learn *"the new song"* which will be played by the heavenly *"harpers"*. Their extraordinary musical ability is demonstrated here as they sing unto the Lord with the scene taking on a holy heavenly aura *"before the throne"* with both heaven and earth harmonizing in instrument and song praising the Lord of the universe for the redemption of His people.

In verse three we are given more specifics: *"which were redeemed from the earth."* The focal point of all Scripture is the word redemption. Here the word emphasizes the Price that was paid for the redemption or buying back of something, which in fact is already owned by God because He created all that exists.

He gave His own Son to buy back, out of the slave market of sin, the souls of men, which He already owned. Underline the Price that was paid, the precious life Blood of Christ! This prize group of men stand upon Mount Zion with the Lamb…one of the first and the last titles given to the Lord Jesus Christ in the New Testament:
"Behold, the Lamb of God that takes away the sin of the world!"
(John 1:29)

"And there shall be no more curse, but, the throne of God and of the Lamb shall be in it." (Revelation 22:3)

The Revelation of Jesus Christ is a book of redemption. No less than twenty-eight times the Lord takes the Old Testament redemption title of *"the Lamb"* in this the final book of Scripture, which has as its emphasis throughout its entirety the glorious topic of redemption.

Then, Revelation 7:4 tells of their undefiled physical purity: *"These are they which were not defiled with women; for they are virgins."* They have given themselves fully to the Lord. They have kept themselves pure physically, thereby lessening one of the great temptations that in the last days of this age will be at the highest level ever, drawing men into sin.

"These are they which follow the Lamb whithersoever He goes." (Revelation14:4b).

This brief but fully descriptive statement indicates their total dedication to the Lord Jesus Christ. "Follow, follow, I will follow Jesus, anywhere, everywhere, I will follow Him" should be the heart-song of all who have been redeemed by the precious Blood of the Lamb.

"These were redeemed from among men, being the first-fruits unto God, and to the Lamb." (Revelation 14:4c)

Here, the same word is used describing their redemption, once again emphasizing the Price paid for their eternal souls. An additional statement reveals their unique position of being *"the first-fruits"* or first to be redeemed under the Old Covenant of that future harvest of Israelites (Romans 11:25, 26) during the 70th Week of Daniel.

Their moral purity is also indicated:
"And in their mouth was found no guile for they are without fault before the throne of God." (Revelation 14:5)

The word *"guile"* lays emphasis on lies or falsehoods. *"Without fault"* indicates their blameless conduct. These men, as part of the believing remnant of Israel *"shall not do iniquity, nor speak lies; neither shall a deceitful tongue be found in their mouth" (Zephaniah 3:13)* thereby providing them with continual abiding access before the throne of God.

This mighty group of end times Disciples of Christ is clearly identified as:
1. Sealed by the Signature of God (7:3)
2. Servants of God (7:3)
3. Sons of Israel (7:4)
4. Standing with the Lamb of God (14:1)
5. Singing a New Song (14:3a)
6. Saved from the Earth (14:3b)
7. Sanctified Physically (14:4a)
8. Surrendered Saints (14:4b)
9. Saved from among Men (14:4c)
10. Saved as the First fruits unto God and The Lamb (14:4d)
11. Sanctified Morally (14:5a)
12. Serving before the Throne of God (14:5b)

In order to fully realize the potential of this magnificent group of disciples of Christ, consider their number, 144 Thousand, revealing that they will be a mighty dynamic force for Christ on earth during the end times when they *"follow Him wherever He goes"*. Remember, they are 12,000 times His original group of twelve disciples *"who turned the world upside down"* at the beginning of this age.

While the known world has exponentially grown since those days, their impact will be tremendously effective indeed for the Gospel of Jesus Christ, during the Great Tribulation (Daniel 11:32-35; 12:3, 10) when they are being prepared for their Day of the Lord Redemption Ministry as the Lord's kingdom of priests.

They will be the instruments of God's mercy to those Jews and Gentiles who will be saved during the closing days of this age and the following time period called *"the great and dreadful Day of the Lord" (Malachi 4:5, 6)*. They will be ready and willing to serve the King of kings, and Lord of lords Who is:
"The Lamb of God Who takes away the sin of the world" (John 1:29)!

The 144 Thousand
The Passing of the Torch - [Part III]

The Lord has given prototypes in the persons of Daniel the prophet and his three companions, Mishael, Azariah, and Hananiah in order to understand more clearly the circumstances and characteristics of the 144 Thousand. These four young men were brought under the authority of a ruthless king when they were taken to Babylon as captives of King Nebuchadnezzar in 606 B.C.

Nebuchadnezzar is a type of the Antichrist as similarities and parallels to the end times can be seen within the historical section (Daniel 1-6) of the book of Daniel. His making of an image and demanding that all of the peoples of the known world fall down and worship it (Daniel 3) is one of the most striking parallels Nebuchadnezzar demonstrates.

This action by Nebuchadnezzar parallels the Antichrist's prophesied end time demand for universal worship, when he also will rule the world and seek to force all to worship his image as recorded in Revelation 13:1-18.

Daniel and his three companions, according to Daniel chapter one where the word eunuch is used to describe the man who was over them *"the prince of the eunuchs"*, were made eunuchs in order to serve in the palace of the king. Their duties included dealing with and being in the presence of the king's wives/women.

It was the prevailing custom for these men to be emasculated in order for them to effectively serve royalty, a custom which continued through New Testament times (Acts 8:27ff). The resulting effect on them is similar to the 144 Thousand who will be called out of every tribe as is indicated in Revelation 14:4 to serve the King of kings: *"These are they which were not defiled with women; for they are virgins."*

These men who will be protected by the Lord during the end times

will be similar to eunuchs. Although not physically emasculated, they will keep themselves physically pure giving their full devotion to the King of kings, the Lord Jesus Christ. The Lord taught a three-fold source of becoming a eunuch in Matthew 19:12:
"For there are some eunuchs, which were so born from their mother's womb: and there are some eunuchs, which were made eunuchs of men; and there be eunuchs, which have made themselves eunuchs for the kingdom of heaven's sake. He that is able to receive it, let him receive it."

Therefore, according to the Lord's teaching a man can become a eunuch:
1. Naturally
2. Man-made
3. Self-made

The 144 thousand are described as men who *"were not defiled with women"* indicating their physical purity belying their choice to fully *"follow the Lamb whithersoever He goes." (Revelation 14:*4) This personal choice amply demonstrates their complete surrender in all things in order to give their lives for the maximum service and glory of their Lord. This is also a fitting description of Daniel, Hananiah, Mishael, and Azariah for these young men recognized early on the call of God on their lives.

The prophecy, which Isaiah pronounced to their great-great-grandfather Hezekiah, king of Judah, could have been known by them for they themselves were *"of the king's seed" (Daniel 1:3).* Isaiah's words spoken to Hezekiah over a century and a half earlier are clear and unmistakable:
"Behold the days come, that all that is in thine house, and that which thy fathers have laid up in store unto this day, shall be carried into Babylon: nothing shall be left, saith the Lord. And of thy sons (Daniel and his four companions) that shall issue from thee, which thou shalt beget, shall they take away; **and they shall be eunuchs in the palace of the king of Babylon.***" (II Kings 20:17, 18)*

These four young men of royalty, who likely had access to the Scriptures, may have known ahead of time some of what God was going to do with them as the king of Babylon closed in on the city of

Jerusalem. He eventually took them captive and enlisted them in his own service as recorded in the book of Daniel 1:1-7.

Their lives and impeccable service to God recorded in the book of Daniel certainly have infinite value for those who follow their pattern of service to their God. There are at least eight similarities or parallels between Daniel and his three companions and the 144 Thousand:
1. They are *"sons of Israel"* (Revelation 7:3; Daniel 2:25)
2. They are called *"servants of God"* (Revelation 7:3; Daniel 3:26)
3. They refuse to be defiled (Revelation 14:4a; Daniel 1:8)
4. They choose to follow God (Revelation 14:4b; Daniel 3:16-18, 28)
5. They refuse to worship an idolatrous image under the threat of death (Revelation 13; Daniel 3)
6. They are without fault (Revelation 14:5; Daniel 6:4)
7. They are seen with the Lord (Revelation 14:1, 17:14; Daniel 3:26, 6:22)
8. They are supernaturally protected by the Lord (Revelation 7:3, 9:4; Daniel 3:23-28, 7:21, 22)

The Lord, being the unchangeable and faithful God that He is, will accomplish these same things in the lives of those He will choose to represent Him during the time of the end. He will prepare this great company of *"servants of our God" (Revelation 7:3)* who will faithfully serve Him during those tumultuous but exciting days ahead.

Regardless of what view/theory is held concerning the timing of the events of the end times, one thing we can rely upon and that is the unchanging faithfulness of our God. He will most certainly call out and prepare that great company of 144 Thousand servants from the twelve tribes of Israel who will:
1. Be the first-fruits of the Jews to be redeemed during the 70th Week of Daniel (Revelation 14:5)
2. Serve the Lord during the Great Tribulation (Daniel 11:32-35, 12:3; Revelation 12:17b)
3. Serve the Lord during the Day of the Lord's wrath (Revelation 7:3-8, 9:4, 14:1-5, 17:14)

The 144 Thousand
The Servants of Our God – As Soldiers

Revelation 17:14 tells of the Lord's end of the age victory: *"These [10 horns/kings] shall make war with the Lamb, and the Lamb shall overcome them: for He is Lord of lords, and King of kings: and **they that are with Him** [144 Thousand] (Revelation 14:1, 4) are called, and chosen, and faithful."*

This brief description of the 144 Thousand warriors shows them as those who are chosen from the twelve tribes and are *"**with the Lamb**...following Him wherever He goes" (Revelation 14:1, 4)..."for many are called, but few are chosen." (Matthew 22:14)*

This verse in Matthew's gospel underlines the meaning of what is said about these choice saints for they are not only called to be the end times warriors but they are also chosen and faithful. While some identify those who are *"called"* to be with the Lord in this verse (Revelation 17:14) as the raptured saints in heaven, the only ones in time of the end Scripture who are clearly shown to be *"with Him"* and *"follow Him wherever He goes"* are the 144 Thousand soldiers of Christ *(Revelation 14:1-5)*.

The word *"faithful"* in Revelation 17:14 really eliminates the glorified saints for faith is no longer necessary when face to face with the Lord in heaven for to be unfaithful is not a possibility for one who is glorified and no longer able to sin.

The faithfulness of the 144 Thousand gives them the desire and ability to *"follow the Lamb whithersoever He goes"* putting them in the midst of the intense warfare which will be waged during the end times. They will become the primary targets of Satan after *"the woman"* [faithful Israel] flees to safety to her place in the wilderness which is prepared by God (Revelation 12:6, 14):
"And the dragon [Satan] was wroth with the woman, and went to make war with the remnant [rest] of her seed [144 Thousand], which keep the commandments of God, and have the testimony of Jesus

Christ." (Revelation 12:17)

The 144 Thousand are the physical warriors who go with the Lord Jesus Christ to battle against the army of the ten horns/kings (Revelation 17:12-14), the *"kings of the east" (Revelation 16:12),* and *"the kings...of the whole world" (Revelation 16:14).* These kings are collectively known as *"the kings of the earth" (Revelation 19:19)* who go to *"the battle of the great day of God Almighty"(Revelation 16:14)* which is the battle of Armageddon.

They will also be active as physical soldiers in Israel during the Antichrist's initial assault upon Jerusalem:
"And this Man [Messiah] shall be the peace, when the Assyrian [Antichrist] shall come into our land: and when he shall tread in our palaces, then shall we raise against him seven shepherds, and eight principal men. And they shall waste the land of Assyria with the sword." (Micah 5:5, 6)

But this is not where their ministry begins. They are present (Revelation 12:17b) during the persecution which intensifies at the mid-point of the 70th Week of Daniel. Then, the Antichrist stops the daily sacrifice and the abomination of desolation [Antichrist's image] is set up in the holy place (Daniel 8:11, 9:27, 11:31, 12:11; Matthew 24:15; II Thessalonians 2:3, 4).

Revelation 12, which focuses on Israel and the Hebrew people, closes with a statement telling of *"the dragon" [Satan]* as he makes *"war with the remnant [rest] of her [The woman/faithful Israel] seed, [the ones which are keeping] the commandments of God and [the ones having] the testimony of Jesus Christ." (Revelation 12:17b)*

The phrase *"of her seed"* indicates the physical seed of the woman and the rest of the verse *"which keep the commandments of God, and have the testimony of Jesus Christ"* shows them as faithful obedient brethren.

This verse points out their physical relationship to *"the woman"*. They are Jews, and their faithful obedience to the Lord during the second half of the 70th Week of Daniel is also clearly indicated. That Satan's persecution will be focused upon these saved Jews indicates that there will also be unsaved Jews who will not be Satan's target. This is indicated in Daniel 11:28-31 where the unsaved Jews collaborate with the Antichrist and *"forsake the holy covenant"* along with still another group of Jews:

"They that understand [the rest of her seed (Revelation 12:17b)] among the people shall instruct many" indicating there will be three different groups of Jews in the land after the abomination of desolation (Daniel 11:31).

This records the continuing assault of Satan on those saved Jews whom God chooses to continue bearing His testimony after *"the woman"*, who represents the faithful of the nation of Israel, flees: *"into the wilderness, into her place, where she is nourished for a time, and times, and half a time [Last 3-1/2 years of Daniel's 70th Week], from the face of the serpent." (Revelation 12:14; Matthew 24:16)*

These young soldiers of Christ will continue to serve Him and their country as every young man in present-day Israel is required to serve in the military. They will remain in the land when *"the woman...flees into her place"*.

Then, Satan's personal attention will be focused upon the earthly people of God, those saved Jews *[they that understand/the rest of her seed]*, who are in the line of fire during the last half of the 70th Week of Daniel. This is when Satan's wrath is at its peak, for *"he knows that he has but a short time" (Revelation 12:12)*.

Daniel 7:21, 25 refers to the same time period assault by the Antichrist upon the Church:
"I beheld, and the same horn [Antichrist] made war with the saints and prevailed against them...And he shall speak great words against the most High, and shall wear out the saints of the most High, and think to change times and laws: and they [the saints] shall be given into his hand until a time and times and the dividing of time [Last 3-1/2 years of Daniel's 70th Week]."

These references are definite indications of the Antichrist's worldwide war upon the saints of the Church for the global scope of

his efforts are recorded:
"The fourth beast...shall be diverse from all kingdoms and shall devour the whole earth, and shall tread it down, and break it in pieces." (Daniel 7:23)

This parallel passage underscores this future global assault upon the Church saints: *"And it was given unto him [Antichrist] to make war with the saints, and to overcome them: and power was given him over all kindreds, and tongues, and nations." (Revelation 13:7)*

Satan, the dragon of Revelation 12, will zero in on the faithful Jews, *"The rest of her seed"*, primarily in the land of Israel. His henchmen, the Antichrist and the false prophet, will conduct a worldwide assault upon the Church saints.

Another passage describing physical warfare at the end of the age is Micah 5:1-9. Through the ages, this powerful Messianic Scripture has been looked to as the renowned passage that predicts the Lord Jesus Christ's birthplace of Bethlehem.

There is more prophetic truth here yet to be fulfilled involving the Messiah during the end times:
"Now muster yourselves in troops (Psalm 110:3), daughter of troops; he [the Antichrist] has laid siege against us; with a rod they will smite the judge of Israel on the cheek. But as for you, Bethlehem, Ephratah, though thou be little among the thousands [clans/military divisions] of Judah, yet out of thee shall He [Messiah] come forth unto Me [Jehovah] to be Ruler in Israel; whose goings forth have been from of old, from everlasting. Therefore, He [Lord] will give them [Israel] up until the time [end of the age] that she [Israel] which travails [time of Jacob's trouble] hath brought forth [all Israel saved]. Then the remnant [rest] of His [Messiah] brethren [the woman/faithful Israel] shall return unto the children [sons] of Israel [144 Thousand]. And He [Messiah] shall stand and feed His flock [All Israel Saved/The Woman/144 Thousand during the Millennium] in the strength of the LORD, in the majesty of the name of the LORD His God. And they [His flock] shall abide, for now shall He [Messiah] be great unto the ends of the earth. And, this Man [Messiah] shall be the Peace, when the Assyrian [Antichrist] shall come into [invades] our land: and when he shall tread [tramples] in our palaces [synagogues], then we

will raise against him seven shepherds and eight principal men. And they shall waste [tend/rule] the land of Assyria with the sword, the land of Nimrod in the entrances thereof; thus shall He [Messiah] deliver us from the Assyrian [Antichrist] when he comes into [attacks] our land and when he treads [tramples] within our borders. And the remnant [144 Thousand] of Jacob shall be in the midst of many people as a dew (Psalm 110:3) from the LORD, as the showers upon the grass, that tarries not for man, nor waits for the sons of men. And the remnant [144 Thousand] of Jacob will be among the Gentiles in the midst of many people as a lion among the beasts of the forest as a young lion among the flocks of sheep: who, if he go through, both treads down and tears in pieces, and none can deliver. Thine hand shall be lifted up upon thine adversaries, and all thine enemies shall be cut off." (Micah 5:1-9)

These nine verses begin with a call for battle preparation: *"Now muster yourselves in troops...He has laid siege against us" (Micah 5:1)* because the Antichrist has come against Jerusalem.

In verse two Bethlehem is described as *"too little"* to be counted among the *"clans"* or military divisions even though it is the birthplace of the Messiah, the Lord Jesus Christ. *"He [the Lord] will give them up"* referring to the setting aside of Israel (Romans 11:8, 25, 26) *"until the time" (Micah 5:3)* when He will thoroughly purge, purify (Jeremiah 30:7; Zechariah 13:9) and redeem Israel at the end of the 70th Week of Daniel (Isaiah 59:20, 21).

There is a *"return to the sons of Israel" (Micah 5:3)* by *"the remainder of His brethren"* indicating the eventual gathering of Jews:
1. The Woman (Revelation 12)
2. The 144 Thousand (Revelation 14:1)
3. The Nation Saved @ End of 70th Week of Daniel (Genesis 49:10, Psalm 102:22; Isaiah 59:20; Daniel 9:24; Hosea 1:11, 3:5; Zechariah 13:8, 9; Romans 11:25, 26; Revelation 11:15, 14:1-5)

These redeemed Jews will gather and eventually populate their promised land during the glorious 1000 year earthly reign of Christ (Revelation 20:1-6) also known as the Millennium. This passage continues describing the Messiah's actions (Micah 5:4, 5a) when the Antichrist enters the land of Israel with his armies after the abomination of desolation and attacks Jerusalem as described in Ezekiel 38, 39; Zechariah 12:1-14, 14:2.

There will be *"seven shepherds and eight principal men" (Micah 5:5b, 6a)* raised against the aggression of the king of Assyria [Antichrist] having great military success as they rule *"the land of Assyria with the sword".*

The Septuagint [Greek Old Testament] translates *"principal men"* as *"attacks of men"* possibly indicating the number of assaults upon the enemy by the seven shepherds. The Hebrew word translated *"principal men"* can also mean *"poured out or libation"* per Strong's lexicon indicating the possibility of the shepherds or rulers seven-fold giving of themselves to the Lord.

The Messiah's deliverance is then recorded:
"Thus shall He deliver us from the Assyrian" (Micah 5:6b) referring to the ultimate victory of the Lord Jesus Christ when He comes as *"King of kings and Lord of lords" (Revelation 19:16).*

Then *"the remnant of Jacob"* [144 Thousand] are once again focused upon in Micah 5:7 where they are a blessing *"in the midst of many people as a dew from the LORD".* This is similar to Psalm 110:3 where they are also referred to as *"dew"* indicating this great multitude of young servants of God.

They will truly be a blessing as they are the instruments of God's divine mercy during the end times when their Redemption Ministry is provided to those who do not know the Lord Jesus Christ as Savior and Messiah. Their ministry is also described in Daniel 11:32-35, 12:3, 10.

The next few verses in Micah 5 illustrate their ferocious prowess as warriors thereby becoming a curse to their enemies:
"And the remnant of Jacob shall be among the Gentiles in the midst of many people as a lion among beasts of the forest, as a young lion among the flocks of sheep: who, if he go through, both treads down and tears in pieces, and none can deliver. Thine hand shall be lifted up upon thine adversaries, and all thine enemies shall be cut off."
(Micah 5:8, 9)

In Micah 5:9 God ends this section with His promise of complete victory to these marvelous soldiers of Christ as they go to battle against the ultimate end times enemy of God. The Antichrist and all the forces he can muster are crushed in his futile attempt to defeat the great and mighty King of Glory.
"Thy people [troops] shall be willing in the day of Thy power [forces/army/battle] in the beauties of holiness [priestly garments] from the womb of the morning, Thou hast the dew of Thy youth [young men]." (Psalm 110:3)

Here the 144 Thousand are described as the Lord's warrior/priests during the Day of His power indicating the Day of the Lord which immediately follows His Second Coming to resurrect, rescue, rapture and receive the saints (Revelation 7:9-17). The theme of Psalm 110 is given in Psalm 110:1:
"Sit thou at My right hand until I make Thy enemies Thy footstool."

The rest of the Psalm shows the LORD Jehovah progressively bringing the Lord Jesus Christ's enemies into submission. This begins with the sending of *"the rod [tribe] of Thy strength"* which refers to the tribe of Judah as the Lord Jesus Christ, *"the Lion of the tribe of Judah" (Revelation 5:5)* will lead His tribe/people in the warfare.

It is during *"the day of His wrath" (Psalm 110:5)* the Day of the Lord, which is described in Psalm 110:5-7 that God supernaturally intervenes with His judgment upon earth and its rebellious inhabitants. Satan unleashes his greatest assault upon the people of God during the last half of Daniel's 70th Week.

Even though Satan will battle with all his might inflicting many casualties among God's people:
"All things work together for good to them that love God to those who are called according to His purpose." (Romans 8:28)

The Lord will use the wickedness of men during the Great Tribulation to purge and purify His Church saints in order *"that He might present it to Himself a glorious church not having spot or wrinkle, nor any such thing but that it might be holy and without blemish." (Ephesians 5:27)*

These soldiers of the Cross, the 144 Thousand, will continue on earth during the Day of the Lord when God purges and purifies His people (Zechariah 13:9). They will provide their Redemption Ministry to those Jews who will be saved at the end of the 70th Week when *"their Redeemer will come to Zion" (Isaiah 59:20) and "all Israel shall be saved." (Romans 11:25, 26)*

The 144 Thousand will remain *"with"* and continue to *"follow the Lamb wherever He goes" (Revelation 14:1, 4, 17:14)* taking part in the army of the Lord Jesus Christ. He will come on His white horse to execute the victory over the kings of the earth, the beast [Antichrist] and the false prophet at the climax of the Day of the Lord, *"the battle of that great day of God Almighty" (Revelation 16:14)*, the battle of Armageddon (Revelation 19:15-21).

The 144 Thousand
The Servants of Our God - As Saviors

During every situation when the Lord delivered His earthly people, the Jews, He used a human mediator, deliverer or savior. Noah brought deliverance for his family before God destroyed the earth (Genesis 6-8) with a universal flood. Abraham provided the necessary mediation to bring about the deliverance of Lot and his family before God destroyed Sodom and Gomorrah (Genesis 18:23-33).

When Israel was in bondage in Egypt, Moses was called by God to be their deliverer, and he went on to minister mightily and was without question Israel's human savior/mediator. He cried out to God on the people's behalf throughout his lengthy forty-year sojourn with the Israelites. During the following time of Joshua, the subsequent series of Judges and Queen Esther the Lord continued this pattern of utilizing a human mediator for the deliverance of His people.

Daniel, although not physically involved in Israel's deliverance from Babylon, nevertheless, he was their spiritual mediator and could even be termed their spiritual deliverer/savior. He prayed mightily to God in chapter nine of his prophecy confessing *"we have sinned"* on four occasions, crying out to God on behalf of his people and himself for forgiveness:
"O Lord, hear, O Lord, forgive; O Lord; hearken and do; defer not for Thine own sake, O my God: for Thy city and Thy people are called by Thy name." (Daniel 9:19)

In like manner, at the time of the end, when God's people are once again in desperate need of deliverance during *"the time of Jacob's trouble" (Jeremiah 30:7)*, God will call out and send, not just one human savior, but, a great company of saviors:
*"And saviors shall come up on mount Zion to judge the mount of Esau; and **the kingdoms shall be the Lords**." (Obadiah 21)*

The time [End of the 70th Week of Daniel] of the fulfillment of this prophecy is indicated in the Revelation: *"And the seventh angel* *sounded; and **the kingdoms of this world are become the kingdoms of our Lord**, and of His Christ; and He shall reign for ever and ever." (Revelation 11:15)*

"And I looked and lo a Lamb stood on mount Zion, and with Him an hundred forty and four thousand, having His Fathers name written in their foreheads." (Revelation 14:1)

These 144 Thousand priests unto God will provide their Redemption Ministry as the end times kingdom of priests which the Lord will use to bring about the spiritual deliverance of their brethren, the nation of Israel *"when all Israel shall be saved" (Romans 11:26).*

The prophet David initially describes them:
"Thy people [troops/prayer warriors] shall be willing in the day of Thy power [army/battle], in the beauties of holiness [priestly garments] from the womb of the morning, Thou hast the dew [multitude] of thy youth [young men]." (Psalm 110:3)

These *"people"* described here are young men adorned with holy character who are the saviors/soldiers in the Lord's army, His priests unto God, the 144 Thousand of the Revelation. This holy company of prayer warriors, who willingly enlist in the Lord's army, are the human instruments God will use to bring into His kingdom that future company of Jews who will be redeemed by The Lamb, The Redeemer, The Messiah, The Lord Jesus Christ, at the end of the 70th Week of Daniel (Isaiah 59:20; Zechariah 13:9; Romans 11:25, 26).

Their position on Mount Zion with the Lamb, the Lord Jesus Christ, worshipping before the throne of God along with the four beasts, the twenty-four elders and the heavenly harpers places them in the presence of God Himself with His Son. This attests to their undefiled, holy condition as indicated in these Scriptures: (Psalm 110:3; Revelation 14:4, 5).

These 144 Thousand *"servants of our God" (Revelation 7:3)* will be responsible during their end times ministry to pray mightily and witness fervently to those whom God will call in that day as the Lord Jesus Christ redeems this great harvest of souls at the end of the 70th Week of Daniel.

The continuation of this most necessary ministry to the lost, which is carried out by the Church saints until they are raptured, will be the major responsibility of these 144 Thousand witnessing warriors of the Lord Jesus Christ. The rapture will occur right after they are sealed guaranteeing the Lord's priesthood and continuing testimony on earth in order for His program of redemption to be carried on during the Day of the Lord which begins the same day the saints are raptured (Luke 17:22-37).

There will be an increasingly intensive spiritual battle for the souls of men (Revelation 12:12) which will be the primary charge of the 144 Thousand fulfilling their calling as witnesses and priests unto God as obedient followers of the Lord Jesus Christ (Revelation 14:4).

As the Lord's mediators, the end times kingdom of priests, they will also have the privilege of fulfilling an important conditional covenant of old:
"Now therefore if ye will obey My voice indeed, and keep My covenant, then ye shall be a peculiar treasure unto Me above all people: for all the earth is Mine. And ye shall be unto Me a kingdom of priests, and an holy nation." (Exodus 19:5, 6).

Although this conditional covenant was never fulfilled due to the disobedience and rebellion of the people of Israel, the end times Israel of God, the 144 Thousand, will indeed bring it to pass. This powerful group of God's servants will in fact minister to the Lord and thereby bring about His will on earth during the Day of the Lord.

It is through powerful prayer and timely witnessing (Daniel 11:33-35, 12:3, 10) that the salvation of the lost will be effected at the end of the age just as it is today. The Lord will continue to be the same *"yesterday, and today and forever" (Hebrews 13:8)* as He calls to Himself those who are written in the Lamb's book of life from the foundation of the world.

He will have His *"saviors" (Obadiah 21),* the end times *"servants of our God" (Revelation 7:3)* who provide their Redemption Ministry being protected (Revelation 3:10, 9:4) and ultimately victorious (Revelation 14:1-5) during the deadly Day of the Lord judgments (Revelation 9:18, 16:3).

The Priesthood of the Apocalypse
Part I

As indicated by their appearance on Mt. Zion with the Lord Jesus Christ, the Lamb, in Revelation 14:1, this group of men provide the fulfillment of a number of important Old Testament prophecies (Genesis 49:10; Psalm 110:3; Obadiah 17-21).

Their first and most significant role of fulfillment is tied to their origin as Hebrew *"servants of our God"* chosen from the twelve tribes of Israel named in Revelation 7:4-8. The list begins with the leader of the tribes, the most heralded son of Jacob, Judah, the one from which God in human flesh, the Messiah, the Lord Jesus Christ would descend (Hebrews 7:14).

Judah, the fourth born son of Leah, Jacob's lawful wife, inherited the position of firstborn. His three older brothers forfeited their right due to their sinful conduct as evidenced by firstborn Reuben's wicked sexual sin (Genesis 35:22) and Simeon and Levi, the second and third born, who brutally slaughtered all the men of Shechem (Genesis 34).

This list of Jacob's sons in Revelation 7:3-8 is similar in structure to the prophecy of Jacob in Genesis 49:1-28 as he first mentions the sons of Leah, then the sons of the two maids, Bilhah and Zilpah, with Rachel's two sons listed last.

Dan, who is replaced by Manasseh, Joseph's oldest son, is the only tribe not seen in the Revelation 7:3-8 list. Ephraim, whose name is absent, is silently represented because his seed are accounted for in the 12,000 sealed under his father Joseph's name as Joseph had only two sons, Manasseh and Ephraim. Therefore, those sealed under Joseph's name are also the descendants of Ephraim.

The 144 Thousand are singled out by their unique position as the only group called the *"first-fruits unto God and unto the Lamb" (Revelation 14:4).* These young men who have been chosen, prepared and physically sealed by God for His divine protection (Revelation 9:4), are the first to be saved, during the restored (Malachi 4:5, 6; Matthew 17:11) *"holy covenant" (Daniel 11:28-31)* dispensation, the 70th Week of Daniel, which is the last week of the seventy weeks that God has determined upon Daniel's *"people" (Daniel 9:24)*.

They are the first of that great company of Israelites who will later be saved when *"the Redeemer [Lord Jesus Christ] comes to Zion" (Isaiah 59:20)* and *"all Israel shall be saved" (Romans 11:26)*.

The 144 Thousand are not just a random group of Israelites chosen to guarantee a remnant to inherit the physical promises given to the Jews under the Old Covenant. No, these men are selected, saved, sealed and serve the King of kings as they *"follow Him wherever He goes" (Revelation 14:4)* showing their full and complete surrender to His will.

One of their likely duties as God's end of the age *"holy nation" (Exodus 19:5, 6; Psalm 110:3; I Peter 2:9; Revelation 14:1-5)*, may be to fulfill the conditional covenant made by God with the nation of Israel in Exodus 19:1-6. when He physically met with the people of Israel as a nation for the first time.

The statement made in Exodus 19:5, 6 shows His intent for the nation and each individual Israelite:
*'Now, therefore, **if** ye will obey My voice indeed, and **keep My covenant**, then ye shall be a peculiar treasure unto Me above all people: for all the earth is Mine. And ye shall be unto me **a kingdom of priests and an holy nation**."*

This conditional covenant made at Mt. Sinai was ultimately broken and left unfulfilled by the disobedience, rebellion, and idolatry of the people of Israel (Exodus 32). However, the Lord Jesus Christ in His full and complete obedience fulfilled the Old Covenant.

His sacrificial death on the Cross paid the penalty for all sin and in reality paid the sin debt for all mankind (I John 2:2). Therefore this broken covenant in fact was atoned for by His once for all sacrifice (Hebrews 10:10, 14).

The importance of this conditional covenant remains intact. God's desire to have this great company of priests ministering to Him continues, (Psalm 110:3; I Peter 2:5, 9; Revelation 1:5; 5:10; 20:6) as the Scripture affirms that there have been *"priests unto God"* ministering to Him and for Him throughout the ages.

He has given each and every new covenant believer the privilege and opportunity to enter into the holiest (Hebrews 10:19) and fulfill this covenant. This was God's original intention and primary calling for each and every person in the nation of Israel just as it now is for each and every born-again believer.

When the Church saints are raptured removing God's priests from the earth and the Day of the Lord judgments begin, the 144 Thousand will remain to perform this most vital ministry. That this great company of 144 Thousand will be holy priests unto God during the Day of the Lord is indicated by their prophetic description:
"Thy people [troops/warrior/priests] shall be willing in the day of Thy power [Day of the Lord] in the beauties of holiness [priestly vestments/garments], from the womb of the morning, Thou hast the dew [multitude] of Thy youth [young men]." (Psalm 110:3)

Based on the position and character of the 144 Thousand as they enter into this unique time of service to God during the Day of the Lord, they can fulfill this broken covenant as they will be serving during a time when they will be protected during the Day of the Lord (Revelation 9:4) *"following the Lamb wherever He goes" (Revelation14: 1-5).*

They will be ministering to and for the Lord, thereby orchestrating the plan of God on earth through powerful praise and intercessory prayer during the most intense spiritual battle of the ages when Satan and his angels are cast down into the earth. (Revelation 12:12)

Psalm 110 is regarded as "The Crown Jewel" of the book of Psalms. This short but powerful revelation by King David provides the believer with marvelous insight concerning David's Lord, the Messiah, the King of kings, our Great High Priest the Lord Jesus Christ.

While it is one of the most quoted passages of Scripture in the New Testament, the important fact here is the One Who quoted its truth as He dealt with the Pharisees concerning His identity as the Messiah, David's Lord and the Son of Jehovah God.

The Lord Jesus referred to this Psalm a number of times during His earthly ministry (Matthew 22:44, 26:64; Mark 12:64, 14:62; 16:19; Luke 20:42, 22:69). It is also utilized over a dozen other times in the New Testament demonstrating its vital importance in the overall scheme of God's unfolding revelation.

The focus in this brief look at Psalm 110 is prophetic, for the majority of the subject matter covered in this Psalm has yet to take place in the course of history. This Messianic Jewel of the Psalms, revealing past and present truth concerning the Lord Jesus Christ, also provides the believer with vital truth in understanding the end times and "<u>The Priesthood of the Apocalypse</u>" as indicated in the Revelation of Jesus Christ in concert with this Psalm.

The coronation of the King of kings, the Lord Jesus Christ is indicated in the opening verse of Psalm 110:
"The LORD said unto my Lord, sit Thou at My right hand until I make Thy enemies Thy footstool."

This clearly underlines Jehovah God's certain intent to give the Lord Jesus Christ eventual physical dominion over the entire earth (Psalm 2:6-9). This first verse also pinpoints the timing of the Psalm as the Lord Jesus Christ has just ascended to heaven (Acts 1:9-11) and is invited by His Father to sit at His right hand.

He sat down at the Father's right hand and was exalted (Acts 2:33) and subsequently sent *"the promise of the Father"*, the Holy Spirit, to His people (Acts 2:1-4) which He promised (Luke 24:49; John 14:16, 17, 26, 15:26, 16:7, 13, 14; Acts 1:4).

The second verse begins the progressive unfolding of end times events which God the Father will bring to pass as He brings Christ's enemies into submission:
"The LORD shall send the rod [tribe] of Thy strength out of Zion, rule Thou in the midst of Thine enemies." (Psalm 110:2)

The phrase *"rod of Thy strength"* some apply to the Church or the Holy Spirit for He was and is now the Person Who empowers and strengthens believers thereby glorifying and exalting the Lord Jesus Christ. He is the Holy Instrument by which Jesus now rules as Lord.

The Church and the Holy Spirit both came *"out of Zion"*, which is the city of Jerusalem, and appear to "fit" the requirements of the passage. However, bringing the Lord Jesus Christ's enemies into submission is not His primary purpose for the Church.

The Church's primary purpose is to be a *"witness"* unto Christ as indicated by the Lord in all five of His commissions: (Matthew 28: 18-20; Mark 16:15; Luke 24:46-48; John 15:16; Acts 1:8) which He gave His disciples and now apply to His Body the Church.

Although it is through the Holy Spirit that God's work and will are now accomplished by the Church, the focus of this Psalm is in the future day when Jehovah God brings into submission the enemies of His Son, not the present-day witnessing of the Church of Jesus Christ.

God will ultimately bring the enemies of the Lord Jesus Christ into submission during His day, the eschatological Day of the Lord. This future end times event is clearly defined in Scripture as it is the most prophesied time in the Word of God.

The Hebrew word "matteh" translated *"rod"* in Psalm 110:2 is found in the Old Testament (251) times with (182) of those occurrences translated *"tribe"*, (52) occurrences translated *"rod"* and (15) times it is translated *"staff"*.

The Theological Wordbook of the Old Testament supplies the following information concerning this word: "Although the term properly means "staff" or "rod," it is usually rendered (some 180 times) "tribe". The reference is usually to one of the twelve tribes by name. At first, apparently, each tribal ruler led his group with a staff. This suggests that the ruler's staff may have originally been a symbol of the tribe (cf. Numbers 17:2-10 [H 17-25] and eventually betokened leadership and authority (cf. Ps 110:2; Jeremiah 48:17)." p.574 Vol.1

Also, the Hebrew word "shebet" a synonym of "matteh" is the word translated "rod" or "scepter" in all of the other Old Testament Messianic passages which speak of the Messiah's rod/scepter (Genesis 49:10; Numbers 24:17; Psalm 2:9, 45:6; Isaiah 11:4).

This is the word the Bible utilizes to define the ruling or smiting of the nations by the Messiah, which will occur during the Day of the Lord. The "shebet" passages above refer to the future rule and the accompanying discipline of the Messiah, the Lord Jesus Christ, when He comes as *"King of kings and Lord of Lords" (Revelation 19:15).*

The phrase *"rod of Thy strength"* might be better translated *"tribe of Thy strength"* indicating the tribe of Judah from which the Lord Jesus Christ descended (Hebrews 7:14). To the tribe of Judah, *"a lion's whelp" (Genesis 49:9)* a prolonged dominion is promised [ISBE p.1738 Vol.3] through the Messiah, so it is listed first in Revelation 7:5 as the leader of the twelve tribes.

Judah will likely lead the assault upon *"the Assyrian" [Antichrist] (Micah 5:5)* not unlike the days during Antiochus Epiphanes [type of Antichrist] similar invasion of Israel in the past (168 B.C.). Then Judas Maccabeus "The Hammer" of the tribe of Judah led his warriors to an incredible and most miraculous victory over Antiochus Epiphanes, the ruthless ruler of that day (I Maccabees).

The Lord Jesus Christ as *"The Lion of the Tribe of Judah" (Revelation 5:5),* will be the Peace for His earthly army in that day. This is indicated in Micah's *"last days" (Micah 4:1)* passage recorded in the second message (Micah 3:1-5:15) of his book, which focuses upon the Coming King, the Lord Jesus Christ:
"And this Man [The Lord Jesus Christ/Messiah] shall be the Peace when the Assyrian shall come into our land: and when he shall tread in our palaces, then shall we raise against him seven shepherds and eight principal men." (Micah 5:5)

"Thy people shall be willing in the day of Thy power, in the beauties of holiness, from the womb of the morning, Thou hast the dew of Thy youth." (Psalm 110:3)

The next period of time immediately following the present age of grace is *"the day of Thy power"* also known as the Day of the Lord, when Christ returns *"in power and great glory" (Matthew 24:30).*

During the Day of the Lord, the Lord Jesus Christ will have *"with Him" (Revelation 14:1, 17:14)* a group of obedient followers (Revelation 14:4) known as these 144 Thousand servants of God.

Psalm 110:3 describes them, providing some distinct qualities and duties of this group of God's servants who "s*hall be willing in the day of Thy [Lord Jesus Christ] power".*

The word *"people" (Psalm 110:3)* appears in the Old Testament over 1800 times and is variously translated. On occasion, as recorded in I Samuel 11 where it is found six times, it has the emphasis of *"troops"* specifically in (v.11) when *"Saul put the people [troops] in three companies"* which is recorded in the Theological Wordbook of the Old Testament p.676 Vol.2 ". There are also a number of passages where the word [people] means 'troops'.

In keeping with the dominating militant theme of this Psalm the NIV gives this interpretation of (Psalm 110:3):
"Your troops shall be willing on your day of battle. Arrayed in holy majesty, from the womb of the dawn you will receive the dew of your youth."

The NASV translates this same verse:
"Thy people will volunteer freely in the day of Thy power; In holy array, from the womb of the dawn, Thy youth are to Thee as the dew."
This version gives an accurate word for word translation of the Hebrew text.

The same willing obedience of the 144 Thousand is recorded in Revelation 14:4 where they *"follow the Lamb wherever He goes"*, having already surrendered themselves to His Lordship long before when they decided to follow Jesus, giving themselves as literal bond-servants of the King of kings (Revelation 7:3).

Their personal holiness before God *"In the beauties of holiness" (Psalm 110:3)* also is confirmed in Revelation 14:4, 5:
"These are they which were not defiled with women...And in their mouth was found no guile: for they are without fault before the

throne of God."

Their physical purity and spiritual holiness affords them the ability to continually *"follow the Lamb"* giving them unbroken access to the throne of God where they fulfill their ministry priority as the end of the age priests unto God, His necessary representatives upon earth..

The last phrase of Psalm 110:3 *"Thou hast the dew of Thy youth"* provides additional information concerning the 144 Thousand. The word *"dew"* most likely indicates their great number, and, as the dew provides refreshment and blessing to the earth, they too, will give these same benefits to those to whom they minister:
*"And the remnant of Jacob shall be in the midst of many people as a **dew** from the Lord, as the showers upon the grass, that tarries not for man, nor waits for the sons of men." (Micah 5:7)*

As priests unto God they will be a blessing direct from God, not dependent on men. The word *"youth"* of Psalm 110:3 is only found in the Old Testament three times with the other two occurrences in Ecclesiastes 11:9, 10:
*"Rejoice, O **young man**, in thy youth; and let thy heart cheer thee in the days of thy youth, and walk in the ways of thine heart, and in the sight of thine eyes; but know thou, that for all these things God will bring thee into judgment. Therefore remove sorrow from they heart, and put away evil from thy flesh: for **childhood** and youth are vanity."*

This word in Psalm 110:3 indicates a designated group of young men, who will be active during the end times, willing to follow the Lord which accurately describes the 144 Thousand.

This also approximates their age and agrees with the tenor of Revelation 14:4 where their virginity is recorded requiring a decision which must be made by these young men early in manhood. The age of twenty was specified in the book of Numbers when the first census was taken for those men who were able and old enough to go to war:
"Take ye the sum of all the congregation of the sons of Israel, after their families, by the house of their fathers, with the number of their names every male by their polls: From twenty years old and upward, all that are able to go forth to war in Israel." (Numbers 1:2, 3)

This indicates the age that will likely determine the lower limit for these soldiers of Christ. They will in fact see spiritual and physical combat as war against the saints occurs during the end times which is clearly indicated in Scripture (Daniel 7:21; Revelation 12:17, 13:7, 17:14, 19:19).

These young men will likely remain in the land as a part of the Israeli army when *"the woman"* [Faithful Israel] of Revelation 12 flees into the wilderness for every young man in present-day Israel is required to serve in the armed forces of their country.

There will be two major assaults against Israel prior to Armageddon with the first beginning at the mid-point of the 70th Week of Daniel which centers upon Judea and the city of Jerusalem (Ezekiel 38:8-16; Daniel 12:1; Matthew 24:15-21).

The second battle will take place in the *"valley of Jehosophat" (Joel 3:1-8; Zechariah 14:1, 2)* with these young men taking part as *"the remnant of Jacob"* when *"the Assyrian [Antichrist] shall come into our land: and when he shall tread in our palaces" (Micah 5:5-8).*

Bible commentator W. Graham Scroggie, D.D. speaks on Psalm 110:3 in his commentary on the Psalms, p.87: "The beauties of holiness..." the reference is to holy attire, holy garments, priestly vestments. The soldiers are priests. The consecrated are warriors. These two sides of Christian calling and character are vitally related. Because we are *"Priests unto God"* we are to *"put on the whole armour of God" (Revelation.1: 6; Ephesians 6:11).* "Thou hast the dew of thy youth" Maclaren translates as "From the womb of the dawn (comes) to Thee the dew of Thy youth (s)"; and he says, 'the principal point of comparison of the army with the dew is probably its multitude.'

From: Spurgeon's Treasury of David
Ver. 3. —The subjects of the Priest King are willing soldiers. In accordance with the warlike tone of the whole Psalm, our text describes the subjects as an army. That military metaphor comes out more closely when we attach the true meaning of the words, "in the day of thy power". The word rendered, and rightly rendered, "power", has the same ambiguity which that word has in the English of the date

of our translation, and for a century later, as you may find in Shakespeare and Milton, who both used it in the sense of "army". Singularly enough we do not employ "powers" in that meaning, but we do another word which means the same thing—and talk of "forces", meaning thereby "troops"..."The day of thy power" is not a mere synonym for "the time of thy might", but means specifically "the day of thine army", that is, "the day when thou dost muster thy forces and set them in array for the war". The King is going forth to conquest. But he goes not alone. Behind him come his faithful followers, all pressing on with willing hearts and high courage. — Alexander McLaren, 1871.

Ver. 3. —Thy people, etc. In homage, they shall be like a company of priests in sacred vestments, for they shall appear "in the beauties of holiness". In number, they shall be like the countless dewdrops "from the womb of the morning", sparkling in the rays of the rising sun, and reflecting his radiance. In glory they shall bear the likeness of Christ's resurrection in all its vernal freshness: "Thou hast the dew of thy youth". —Benjamin Wildon Cart.

Ver. 3. —In the beauties of holiness. In holy vestments as priests. They are at once warriors and priests; meet for the service of Him who was King and Priest. Neander (Mem. of Chr. Life, ch. 4) remarks on the connection between these two sides of the Christian character. God's soldiers can only maintain their war by priestly self-consecration. Conversely: God's priests can only preserve their purity by unintermitted conflict. —William Kay.

Ver. 3. —In the beauties of holiness. This expression is usually read as if it belonged either to the words immediately proceeding, or to those immediately following. In either case the connection is somewhat difficult and obscure. It seems better regarded as a distinct and separate clause, adding a fresh trait to the description of the army. And what that is we need not find any difficulty in ascertaining. "The beauties of holiness" is a frequent phrase for the sacerdotal garments, the holy festal attire of the priests of the Lord. So considered, how beautifully it comes in here. The conquering King whom the psalm hymns is a Priest forever; and an army of priests follows him. The soldiers are gathered in the day of the muster, with high courage and willing devotion, ready to fling away their lives; but they are clad not in mail, but in priestly robes; like those who wait before the altar rather than like those who plunge into the fight, like those who compassed Jericho with the ark for their standard and the trumpets for all their weapons. We can scarcely fail to remember the words, which echo these and interpret them. "The armies which were in heaven followed him on white horses, clothed in fine linen, white and clean" —a strange armor against sword cut and spear thrust. —Alexander McLaren.

Ver. 3. —Thou hast the dew of thy youth. These words are often misunderstood, and taken to be a description of the fresh, youthful energy attributed by the Psalm to the Priest King of this nation of soldier priests. The misunderstanding, I suppose, has led to the common phrase, "the dew of one's youth". The reference of the expression is to the army, not to its leader. "Youth" here is a collective noun, equivalent to "young men". The host of his soldier subjects is described as a band of young warriors, whom he leads, in their fresh strength and countless numbers and gleaming beauty like the dew of the morning... It is as a symbol of the refreshing which a weary world will receive from the conquests and presence of the King and his host, that they are likened to the glittering morning dew. Another prophetic Scripture gives us the same emblem when it speaks of Israel being "in the midst of many people as a dew from the Lord". Such ought to be the effect of our presence. We are meant to gladden, to adorn, and to refresh this parched, prosaic world, with freshness brought from the chambers of the sunrise. —Alexander McLaren.

Matthew Henry writes-p.660 'That they should be a willing people, a people of willingness, alluding to servants that choose their service and are not coerced to it…to soldiers that are volunteers and not pressed men…That they should be so in the day of His power, in the day of Thy muster (so some) when Thou art enlisting soldiers thou shalt find a multitude of volunteers…Or when Thou art drawing them out to battle they shall be willing to *"follow the Lamb whithersoever He goes" (Revelation 14:4).'*

W. Graham Scroggie, William Kay, Alexander McLaren, and Matthew Henry all see the "people" here in Psalm 110:3 as soldiers of the Lord's army with most of these commentators also giving them the duty of priests. Matthew Henry also indicates the 144 Thousand are willing to *"follow the Lamb whithersoever He goes." (Revelation 14:4)*

This future army of the King of kings will be completely submissive to the will of God during the Day of the Lord. These young soldiers of Christ will be involved in the intense spiritual warfare at the end of the age as priests unto God. They will be arrayed in holiness doing the Lord's service *"before the throne of God" (Revelation 14:1, 4).*

These "priests unto God" are involved in this future holy warfare when the battle is at its most heightened level, when Satan "knows that he has but a short time" (Revelation 12:12).

Scroggie, in his commentary on the Psalms, adds "Messiah's soldiers are declared to be priests (Psalm 110:3) before His own priesthood is announced." p.88.

In Psalm 110:4 David continues to address the Lord Jesus Christ telling Him of His eternal priesthood which is pronounced by Jehovah:
"The LORD hath sworn and will not repent, Thou art a priest forever after the order of Melchizedek."

The LORD Jehovah, told Jesus of His future actions in Psalm 110:2, 3 before He declared the Lord Jesus Christ's present High Priestly office in Psalm 110:4, remembering that the Psalm (Psalm 110:2-4) is addressing the Lord Jesus after He ascended to heaven.

Jehovah in Psalm 110:4 takes an oath and tells of Jesus' present ministry to the Father and the people as: *"He ever lives to make intercession for those who come unto God by Him." (Hebrews 7:25)*

The consecration of our Great High Priest King is accomplished in this the key verse of Psalm 110 being thoroughly explained in the book of Hebrews chapters 2-9. However, our focus here is on the 144 Thousand and in (v.5-7) they are directly addressed:
"The Lord at thy right hand shall strike through kings in the day of His wrath."(Psalm 110:5)

Here, the people [troops/priests/144 Thousand] (Psalm 110:3) are given the promise of the Lord's presence *"at thy right hand"* when He pours out His devastating wrath upon the earth dwellers during the

Day of the Lord.

This agrees with Revelation 6:16, 17:
"From the wrath of the Lamb: For the great day of His wrath is come; and who is able to stand?"

Although the Day of the Lord is described as the wrath of God (Isaiah 13:9; Zephaniah 1:15), in the first reference to wrath in the book of the Revelation it is also designated *"the wrath of the Lamb"*.

The overriding tone of Psalm 110 is one of dominion, troops, warfare and human carnage which is brought on by the Lord's judgment of earth through the outpouring of His eschatological Day of the Lord/ *"day of His wrath" (Psalm 110:5)*. This couples accurately with the warfare and judgment thoroughly detailed in the Revelation of Jesus Christ (Revelation 8, 9, 15-19).

Notice, the word *"Lord"* [Adonai] *(Psalm 110:5)* continues to refer to the Lord Jesus Christ, as in Psalm 110:1. This promise of the Lord's presence with His people as indicated by His *"right hand"* is found in the Psalms twenty one times and refers to the power, authority and blessing of the Lord to His people in nineteen of these occurrences.

Here, the promise of the blessed presence of the Lord Jesus Christ is given when *"this Man [Messiah] will be the peace" (Micah 5:5)* for those who will be *"with Him" (Revelation 14:1, 17:14)* during *"the day of His wrath" (Psalm 110:5)*.

Psalm 110:6 vividly portrays the Divine Judge's wrath as it is poured out upon earth:
"He shall judge among the heathen, He shall fill the places with the dead bodies, He shall wound the heads [kings of the earth] over many countries."

His Day of the Lord judgment includes the death of over one third of the world population (Revelation 9:15, 16:3) and the final event of the Day of the Lord, the battle of Armageddon, will execute deadly judgment upon the *"kings of the earth" (Revelation 19:19-21)*.

The closing verse pictures the Lord Jesus Christ's actions and attitude of complete victory after the Day of the Lord's wrath is ended:
"He shall drink from the brook in the way, therefore shall He lift up the head." (Psalm 110:7)

The Lord is physically refreshed and assumes the well-deserved appearance and expression of His triumphant victory after His work of judgment is over, after the climactic battle of Armageddon (Revelation 19:11-21) has ended.

This brief Psalm comes to a quiet close after covering the time from the Lord's ascension to the Father's right hand, moving over the present Church age in order to focus completely on the great and dreadful Day of the Lord when God the Father will make the Lord Jesus Christ's enemies His footstool.

While the emphasis is upon the Messiah, the Lord Jesus Christ and His eternal position of Great High Priest, much additional information is given concerning *"Thy people...thy youth"*, those who will be the Lord's loyal subjects during those coming days at the time of the end:
1. They are willing servants. (Psalm 110:3; Revelation 7:3, 14:4, 5)
2. They minister during *"The day of Thy power"*/Day of the Lord. (Psalm 110:2, 3; Revelation 9:4, 14:1, 17:14)
3. They are holy priests/warriors. (Psalm 110:3; Revelation 14:4, 5)
4. They will be refreshing *"as dew"* to Israel/God's people. (Psalm 110:3; Micah 5:7; Revelation 14:4, 5)
5. They will be destructive *"as lions"* to Gentiles/earth dwellers. (Micah 5:8; Revelation 17:14)
6. They will be a great multitude *"as dew"*. (Psalm 110:3; Revelation 7:3-8)
7. They will be young Hebrew men. (Psalm 110:3; Revelation 7:3)

These young men will play a key role during the days leading up to the time of their sealing. Daniel chapter seven tells of the saints being *"given into the hand" (Daniel 7:25)* of the Antichrist. He makes *"war with the saints"* and *"prevails against them" (Daniel 7: 21)* wearing out the saints (Daniel 7:25) for a period of three and one half years which is also indicated in Revelation 13:7.

This intense time of persecution will be unparalleled (Matthew 24:21) and the Redemption Ministry of this mighty kingdom of priests, the 144 Thousand, during that time will be a vital part of the Lord's protection for the saints on earth in an hour when Satan's wrath will be at its maximum strength. (Revelation 12:12)

This theory is based upon the 144 Thousand being Old Covenant believers *"redeemed from the earth...and from among men" (Revelation 14:3, 4).*

Their first priority is to fulfill the primary purpose and calling of every New Testament believer, which is to be a priest unto God (I Peter 2:5, 9; Revelation 1:5, 5:10).

This is the focus of the believer's service and is listed in conjunction with redemption on two occasions (Revelation 1:5, 5:10) indicating that the primary purpose for redemption itself is the creation of a great company of priests unto God, for ministry to Him and men on His behalf.

They also represent the nation of Israel. As the Lord begins to again deal with Israel during the 70th Week of Daniel the restored (Matthew 17:11) *"holy covenant" (Daniel 11:28-32)* economy will once again prevail, just as it was in effect during the first 69 Weeks of this period of 70 Weeks that God has determined upon His people and upon His holy city. (Daniel 9:24)

This single theory based on Bible truth provides the answer to the questions: Why did not the 144 Thousand, and *"the woman"* [Faithful Israel] of Revelation 12, and the *"two witnesses"* of Revelation 11 get caught up together with the other saints when the Lord Jesus Christ came in the clouds?

One possibility is that they were saved under the Old Covenant and were not sealed by the Holy Spirit as New Covenant believers but were physically sealed with the name of God and the Lamb in their foreheads. Therefore they may not have the *"earnest of their inheritance" (Ephesians 1:13, 14),* the indwelling Holy Spirit.

Another possibility is that the Lord has simply chosen to select certain of His earthly people, the Jews, to remain and accomplish His purposes during His Day of the Lord wrath.

Then, He will execute *"the time of Jacob's trouble" (Jeremiah 30:7)* which is specifically designed to purge and purify those Jews (Zechariah 13:9) who will be saved when their Redeemer comes to Zion (Isaiah 59:20; Romans 11:25, 26) at the end of the 70th Week (Revelation 11:15, 14:1).

"The woman" [Faithful Israel] of Revelation 12 will be fed and nourished in the wilderness during the last half of Daniel's 70th Week. The *"two witnesses"* of Revelation 11:3-14 will minister during the last half of Daniel's 70th Week and the 144 Thousand will perform their Redemption Ministry during those same 3-1/2 years (Revelation 7:3-8, 9:4, 14:1-5).

All of these faithful Jews will remain on earth after the resurrection of the dead in Christ and the rapture of the living saints (I Thessalonians 4:16, 17). This end times timeline is based upon the chronological order of events (Matthew 24:3-31) the Lord Jesus Christ clearly gave to *"Peter and James and John and Andrew" (Mark 13:3),* His inner circle of disciples.

This also answers the question concerning the saints who are given into the hand of the Antichrist (Daniel 7:25) for 3-1/2 years which is the last half of Daniel's 70th Week. These Jews will be saved under the Old Covenant and might not be sealed with the Holy Spirit.

They will be purposely left behind to serve the Lord during the *"time of Jacob's trouble"* which occurs during the seven trumpet judgments (Revelation 8:1-11:19) at the beginning of the *"great and dreadful Day of the Lord" (Malachi 4:5, 6).*

The 70th Week of Daniel will, just as the other dispensations, transition or merge into effect with the confirming of the covenant by the many of Israel and the Antichrist (Daniel 9:27) as the actual starting point, just as the Day of Pentecost in Acts 2 became the actual starting point of the dispensation of grace.

But, there was a merging of economies as John the Baptist

preached and the Lord's earthly ministry unfolded and then the Old Covenant continuing to operate after Pentecost in practice by the Jews while the New Covenant was in fact fully effective and functioning on the Day of Pentecost.

This merging of economies has been the Lord's pattern throughout the ages as the economy of Conscience, Human Government, Promise and Law also transitioned into effect with all of them continuing to run in the background still having effect in principle even now as the ages roll.

We also must keep in mind that when the majority of the New Testament was written the required elements were in place in order for the Lord to return. The Jews were in the land, as a people/nation, they occupied Jerusalem, the temple was on Mount Zion, and the Old Covenant with the sacrificial system was operating.

These conditions definitely influenced the anticipation for the Lord's Second Coming by the Early Church, and caused an intense urgency in the believers to expect the Lord's coming post-haste. They correctly viewed the prophetic Scriptures and understood the possibility for the Lord to return in that day as the above prerequisites were in place.

When all five of these prerequisites were brought to their end in A.D. 70 by the Roman army's decimation of the Jews as a people, the complete destruction of the temple and the city of Jerusalem, Israel as a nation and the Old Covenant practices with its sacrificial system were also brought to their conclusion.

However, the Apostle John's inspired writings (The Gospel of John, I, II, III John, Revelation) were all written **after** the destruction of Jerusalem in 70 A.D. and the dispersion of the Jews.

These books of the Bible authored by John between A.D. 80-95 do not echo the same urgency as the epistles of Paul and Peter concerning the Lord's Coming for John knew that the above prerequisites were necessary in order for the Lord to return in that day.

At this present time [2009] three of the above five elements are now back in place. Therefore, we must ever be aware of exactly where we stand in this day as the merging of this last "Jewish" economy has begun for the Jews are a people, in the land, and occupy their holy city Jerusalem.

These prophesied events are the first three prerequisites in order for the 70th Week of Daniel to begin and the Lord Jesus to return (Deuteronomy 30:3-5; Daniel 9:24). The following list shows those prerequisites mentioned above and includes a number of other events required for the *"time of the end/70th Week of Daniel"* to unfold:
1. The Jews will be a "*people*"/nation (Daniel 9:24)
2. The Jews will be in their promised "*land*" (Deuteronomy 30:5; Matthew 24:16)
3. The Jews will occupy their "*holy city*" Jerusalem (Daniel 9:24)
4. The prophet Elijah will be sent to "*restore all things*" (Malachi 4:5, 6; Matthew 17:11; Mark 9:12)
5. The "*holy covenant*" will be restored (Daniel 11:28-32)
6. "*The temple of God*" will be rebuilt (Daniel 11:31; II Thessalonians 2:1-4; Revelation 11:1, 2)
7. The "*holy place*" will be included (Matthew 24:15)
8. The "*regular/daily sacrifices*" will be instituted (Daniel 8:11, 12, 9:27, 11:31, 12:11)
9. The Jews will "*worship*" in the temple of God (Revelation 11:1.2)
10. "*The Sabbath*" will be honored (Matthew 24:20)
11. The sending of prophets to the people of God will occur (Malachi 4:5, 6; Matthew 17:11; Revelation 11:3-14)
12. "*The twelve tribes of Israel*" will be recognized (Revelation 7:4-8)

Also, the Lord's prophecy concerning the *"beginning of sorrows" (Matthew 24:8)* has already begun to take place as the 19th century witnessed the most massive influx of *"false Christs"* with the birth and rise of these major 'Christian' cults:
1. The Jehovah 'false' Witnesses
2. The Mormons/Latter Day 'false' Saints
3. The Seventh Day Adventists
4. The Christian Science 'false' Church

The last half of the 19th century, along with the first half of the 20th

saw USA's Civil War, World War I, World War II and numerous other wars/conflicts across the globe. This defines the period of *"wars and rumors of war" (Matthew 24:6).*

The last part of the 20th century, and now, the beginning of the 21st reveal that we are nearing the very end of the *"the beginning of sorrows"* as increasing *"famines [40 countries recording mass starvation] and pestilences [AIDS, Ebola, Avian Flu, SARS, Swine flu etc.] and [major and numerous] earthquakes"* are evident and continue to rise in magnitude, intensity and number. (Matthew 24:5-8)

Lest this may sound as though anticipation for the soon coming of the Lord is waning, it is a certain and indisputable fact that God is able to bring about the necessary conditions and events *"quickly"* (Revelation 22:20), in His perfect timing, just as He wills.

The expectation for the return of the Lord Jesus Christ, during this very *"generation"* when *"all these things" (Matthew 24:33, 34)* are surely coming to pass, will continue to be on high alert, until we see Him ***"in the clouds"****(Daniel 7:13; Matthew 24:30; Acts 1:9-11; I Thessalonians 4:17; Revelation 1:7).*

The Priesthood of the Apocalypse
Part II

In order to understand how the priesthood will function during the time of the end it will be necessary to briefly review the priesthood in Scripture beginning with the first *"priest"*:

"And the king of Sodom went out to meet him [Abram] after his return from the slaughter of Chedorlaomer, and of the kings that were with him, at the valley of Shaveh, which is the king's dale. And Melchizedek king of Salem brought forth bread and wine: and he was **the priest of the most high God***. And he blessed him, and said, Blessed be Abram of the most high God, possessor of heaven and earth: And blessed be the most high God, which has delivered thine enemies into thy hand. And he [Abram] gave him [Melchizedek] tithes of all." (Genesis 14:17-20)*

While Melchizedek is the first priest to appear in the Scriptures, the primary purpose for his appearance is to exalt God the Son, the Lord Jesus Christ who is our Great High Priest. This Melchizedek is a type of the Lord Jesus Christ, Who became God's Personal Priest when He gave His life and shed His Blood on the Cross as God's Personal Sacrifice for the sin of mankind:

"For all have sinned and come short of the glory of God; Being justified freely by His grace through the redemption that is in Christ Jesus: Whom God has set forth to be a propitiation through faith in His Blood, to declare His righteousness for the remission [forgiveness] of sins that are past through the forbearance of God; To declare, I say, at this time His righteousness: that He might be just, and the Justifier of him who believes in Jesus." (Romans 3:23-27)

The Lord Jesus, as *"the Lamb of God" (John 1:29)*, was the only one Who could satisfy the demands of a righteous, holy God Who needed this *"holy, harmless, undefiled, separate from sinners, and made higher than the heavens" (Hebrews 7:26)* Lamb of God to be His Sacrifice that He might be able to present every man with His loving mercy found only in His Son, the Lord Jesus Christ!

The Lord Jesus Christ's priesthood is clearly announced by God:
"The LORD has sworn and will not repent, Thou [Lord Jesus Christ] art a priest forever after the order of Melchizedek." (Psalm 110:4)

This Psalm of David has as its pivotal verse the celebrated proclamation of God the Father to His Son after the Lord Jesus Christ's *"once for all" (Hebrews 10:10)* sacrifice on the Cross:
"But this Man, after He had offered one sacrifice for sins for ever, sat down on the right hand of God; From henceforth expecting till His enemies be made His footstool." (Hebrews 10:12, 13)

Therefore, the timing of this statement by God in Psalm 110:4 is fixed for it occurs right after the Lord Jesus Christ ascended to heaven to present His precious Blood to His Father in heaven:
"But Christ being come an High Priest of good things to come, by a greater and more perfect tabernacle, not made with hands, that is to say, not of this building; Neither by the blood of goats and calves, but by His own Blood, He entered in once into the holy place, having obtained eternal redemption for us. For if the blood of bulls and of goats, and the ashes of and heifer sprinkling the unclean, sanctifies to the purifying of the flesh: How much more shall the Blood of Christ, Who through the eternal Spirit offered Himself without spot to God, purge your conscience from dead works to serve the living God?" (Hebrews 9:11-14)

The opening verse of Psalm 110 also determines the topic or theme of this powerful jewel of the Messianic Psalms as God pronounces His intent and purpose of making the enemies of the Lord Jesus Christ His footstool.

However, Christ's enemies will not be made His footstool until the great Day of the Lord (Isaiah 2:11-21) which is when God will pour out His wrath (Revelation 6:12-17) upon the enemies of Christ. This wrath of God is detailed in the Seven Trumpet Judgments, the Seven Seal Judgments, the destruction of Babylon and the Battle of Armageddon (Revelation 8-19).

The remainder of Psalm 110 continues this prophetic theme by skipping over the ages in between the time the Lord Jesus Christ is seated at the Father's right hand in verse one and proceeds immediately to the end times when God will *"send the rod [tribe] of Thy strength out of Zion" (Psalm 110:2).*

The Lord Jesus Christ as *"the Lion of the tribe of Judah" (Revelation 5:5)* will *"rule in the midst of His enemies" (Psalm 110:2)* as He *"shall be the Peace when the Assyrian [Antichrist] shall come into our land: and when he shall tread in our palaces"(Micah 5:5)* in that future day.

This end times conflict in the land will occur right after the *"abomination of desolation"* spoken of by Daniel the prophet (Daniel 11:31) and the Lord Jesus Christ (Matthew 24:15).

The Lord Jesus gives His people in the land of Judea this pointed instruction in the very next verse:
"Then let them which be in Judea flee into the mountains."
(Matthew 24:16)

Although this command is given to the faithful in Judea, it applies to all born again believers world wide for this intense persecution called *"great tribulation" (Matthew 24:21)* will come upon all saints as the Antichrist's *"war with the saints" (Daniel 7:21; Revelation 13:7)* will be global in scope.

This flight of the faithful in the land of Israel is also recorded in the book of the Revelation as Satan's focus will be upon the holy land and the city of Jerusalem::
"And the woman fled into the wilderness where she has a place prepared of God, that they should feed her there a thousand two hundred and three score days…And to the woman were given two wings of a great eagle, that she might fly into the wilderness, into her place, where she is nourished for a time, and times, and half a time, for the face of the serpent." (Revelation 12:6,14)

However, there will be certain faithful Jews who remain:
"And the dragon was wroth with the woman, and went to make war with the remnant [rest] of her seed which keep the commandments of God and have the testimony of Jesus Christ." (Revelation 12:17)

This group called the *"remnant of her seed"* also appears in

Daniel's prophecy:

"*But **the people that do know their God** shall be strong and do exploits. And **they that understand among the people** shall instruct many: yet they shall fall by the sword, and by flame, by captivity, and by spoil, many days. Now when they shall fall they shall be helped with a little help: but many shall cleave to them with flatteries. And some of them of understanding shall fall, to try them, and to purge, and to make them white, even to the time of the end: because it is yet for a time appointed.*" *(Daniel 11:32-35)*

These Jews in the land who *"know their God"* will minister to their brethren during the time which follows the *"abomination of desolation"* *(Daniel 11:31, Matthew 24:15).*

Many will fall as martyrs (Revelation 6:9-11, 12:11, 20:4) during the Antichrist's vicious persecution until the appointed *"time of the end" (Daniel 11:35)* when the *"great tribulation"* is cut short (Matthew 24:21) and *"then shall the end [day of the Lord] come" (Matthew 24:14).*

Then, those *"servants of our God" (Revelation 7:3)* that remain will be sealed (Revelation 7:1-8) and continue their ministry during the Day of the Lord as God's *"royal priesthood" (I Peter 2:9)* continues **after** the saints are raptured (I Thessalonians 5:13-18) and received in heaven (John 14:3; Revelation 7:9-17).

These 144 Thousand priests unto God are described in Psalm 110:3 the verse just before God's announcement of the Lord Jesus Christ's priesthood:

"*Thy [Christ's] people shall be willing in the day of Thy power [Day of the Lord], in the beauties of holiness [priestly garments] from the womb of the morning Thou hast the dew of Thy youth [young men]." (Psalm 110:3)*

The priesthood which began with Melchizedek in Genesis 14 continued as God's people, the Jews, progressively grew in size for there were priests among the Israelites after they came out of Egypt when the total number of Israelites is estimated to be approximately 1.5 million:

"*And let **the priests** also, which come near to the LORD, sanctify* *themselves, lest the LORD break forth upon them…And the LORD said unto him [Moses], Away get thee down, and thou shall come up, thou, and Aaron with thee: but let not **the priests** and the people break through to come up unto the LORD, lest He break forth upon them." (Exodus 19:22,24)*

However, under Moses' leadership, God revealed His desire for a major expansion of the priesthood when He explained:
*"Now therefore, if ye will obey My voice indeed, and keep My covenant then ye shall be a peculiar treasure unto Me above all people: for all the earth is Mine: And ye shall be unto me a **kingdom of priests** and an holy nation. These are the words which thou shall speak unto the children of Israel." (Exodus 19:5,6)*

This covenant foreshadows the priesthood blessing (I Peter 2:5, 9) given to every new covenant believer in Christ. But, Israel as a people/nation, did not obey God even though they expressed their good intentions immediately after Moses gave them these Words from God:
"And Moses came and called for the elders of the people, and laid before their faces all these Words which the LORD commanded him. And all the people answered together, and said, All that the LORD has spoken we will do" (Exodus 19:7,8)

But, their bent toward idolatry became evident shortly thereafter when:
"Moses delayed to come down out of the mount, the people gathered themselves together unto Aaron, and said unto him, Up make us gods, which shall go before us; for as for this Moses, the man that brought us up out of the land of Egypt, we know not what is become of him." (Exodus 32:1)

Aaron fashioned a golden calf from the people's jewelry and then declared: *"These be thy gods" (Exodus 32:4)* which eventually caused God to judge the rebellious people:
" And he said unto them, Thus saith the LORD God of Israel, Put every man his sword by his side, and go in and out from gate to gate throughout the camp, and slay every man his brother, and every man his companion, and every man his neighbor. And the children of Levi did according to the Word of Moses: and there fell of the people that

day about three thousand men." (Exodus 32:27, 28)

Aaron, Moses older brother, was the first high priest of the Levitical priesthood, which began with God's appointment of Aaron and his four sons:
"And take thou unto thee Aaron thy brother, and his sons with him, from among the children of Israel, that he may minister unto Me in **the priest's** *office, even Aaron, Nadab and Abihu, Eleazar and Ithamar, Aarons's sons." (Exodus 28:1)*

This priesthood continued for over 900 years until Solomon's temple in Jerusalem was destroyed by Nebuchadnezzar and the people were carried away to Babylon in 586 B.C.

However, when they returned to the land and rebuilt the temple after their seventy-year captivity the Levitical priesthood once again was back in operation:
"And the children of Israel, **the priests***, and the Levites and the rest of the children of the captivity, kept the dedication of this house of God with joy." (Ezra 6:16)*

The temple in Jerusalem was destroyed again about 600 years later which was foretold by the Lord Jesus Christ:
"And Jesus went out, and departed from the temple: and His disciples came to Him for to show Him the buildings of the temple. And Jesus said unto them, See ye not all these things? Verily I say unto you, There shall not be left here one stone upon another, that shall not be thrown down. (Matthew 24:1,2)

This destruction occurred in 70 A.D. by the Roman armies of Titus about 40 years after the Lord Jesus Christ spoke these prophetic words:
"And when ye shall see Jerusalem compassed with armies, then know that the desolation thereof is nigh" (Luke 21:20)

During this time the Romans slaughtered multitudes of Jews and took many captives:
"And they shall fall by the edge of the sword, and shall be led away captive into all nations: and Jerusalem shall be trodden down of the Gentiles, until the times of the Gentiles be fulfilled." (Luke 21:24)

When the temple was destroyed the Levitical priesthood came to an end. But, in recent days, almost 2,000 years later, there is a movement within the land of Israel to restore the priesthood which will definitely be in operation during the 70th Week of Daniel when *"the daily sacrifice" (Daniel 8:11,13,26, 9:27, 11:31)* will once again be offered and the Jews will worship in the 70th Week temple of God: *"And there was given me a reed like unto a rod: and the angel stood saying, Rise, and measure **the temple of God**, and the altar, and them [the Jews] that worship therein. But the court which is without the temple leave out, and measure it not; for it is given unto the Gentiles: and the holy city shall they tread under foot forty and two months." (Revelation 11:2)*

Therefore, what began with Melchizedek has progressed throughout the pages of Scripture with the present-day priesthood made up of born-again believers. They are currently the mediators between God and man under the headship of the Lord Jesus Christ who is our Great High Priest in the heavenlies.

When the saints are raptured, the majority of God's mediators will be removed from the earth. Then, the 144 Thousand sealed *"servants of our God"(Revelation 7:3)*, who are described in Psalm 110:3 as priests, will remain (Revelation 9:4) and continue their ministry during the Day of the Lord (Revelation 9:4; 14:1-5, 17:14) as the Lord's *"holy priesthood…a royal priesthood, and holy nation"* (I Peter 2:5,9). Therefore, the 144 Thousand who are sealed from the twelve tribes of Israel will continue their Redemption Ministry on earth and become:

"The Priesthood of the Apocalypse"

Herein lies the primary purpose for these 144 Thousand young men. For, one of the primary purposes in redemption itself is the creation of a *"**kingdom of priests**" (Revelation 1:5, 6, 5:9, 10) t*o go forth as the Lord's army of mediators throughout the earth representing God to man and man to God!

Someone has rightly said: "Prayer is the battle, the ministry is but the picking up of the spoils". And, it is this Holy Spirit-led praying by the priest unto God that wins the battle for the souls of men.

This enables the priest unto God, as they enter the battlefield daily, to "pick up the spoils" i.e. those souls to whom the Spirit of Christ leads as the believer-priest becomes their mediator before God's throne!

This is the primary work of the priest unto God! The time the priest spends on their knees preparing their daily battlefield by kneeling at the foot of the Cross which is the priest's *"altar" (Hebrews 13:10), seeking the kingdom (Luke 12:31,32), confessing sin (I John 1:9), casting down imaginations and every high thing that exalts itself against the knowledge of God, bringing into captivity every thought to the obedience of Christ (II Corinthians 10:3-5)* is of utmost importance in order for the Lord to win the battle in the heavenlies and accomplish His will upon earth.

This preparation of the heart and mind of the priest formulates the basis for the daily victories won in the lives of those to whom the believer-priest is led by the Holy Spirit.

This is and will continue to be the battle plan for the obedient priest unto God who is militantly victorious in the heavenly conflict which will continue to rage on until the last soul is won for the glory of the Lord Jesus Christ!

This is a simple but undoubtedly the only effective plan of attack for every priest unto God just as the Lord Himself gave the example: *"And in the morning, rising up a great while before day, He went out, and departed into a solitary place, and there prayed." (Mark 1:35)*

Although He was God in the flesh, He still practiced the discipline of praying to His Father thereby receiving His marching orders as it were for the upcoming day because He also was fully Man.

Yes, *"God was in Christ reconciling the world unto Himself" (II Corinthians 5:19)*, but, it was still necessary for Him as the God Man to commune with *"Our Father which art in heaven" (Matthew 6:9)*.

Therefore, our *"Great High Priest" (Hebrews 4:14)* set the perfect example for us during His earthly ministry in order that we might look *"unto Jesus" (Hebrews 12:2)* as we minister as priests unto God during our time here for *"we have this treasure in earthen vessels that the excellency of the power may be of God, and not of us"* (II Corinthians 4:7)

After their Redemption Ministry during the Apocalypse is complete, the 144 Thousand priests unto God will enter the Millennium which is the 1,000 year time period recorded in (Revelation 20:1-6). This is when the Lord Jesus Christ will physically reign upon earth from David's throne in the city of Jerusalem (Isaiah 9:6, 7; Luke 1:32).

However, two other groups of Israelites will also join the 144 Thousand to populate the land of Israel during that same time as outlined by Micah the prophet:
"Therefore will He [Messiah] give them [Israel] up until the time [End of 70th Week] that she [Israel] which travails [during the time of Jacob's trouble] (Jeremiah 30:7) has brought forth: [all Israel shall be saved] (Isaiah 59:20; Romans 11:25,26) then the remnant [rest] of His [Messiah's] brethren [the woman] (Revelation 12:1,6,14) shall return unto the sons of Israel [144 Thousand]." (Micah 5:3)

After the 70th Week temple in Jerusalem is destroyed during the Day of the Lord another temple will be built during the Millennium which is documented in Ezekiel 40-42. Then, the Levitical priesthood will be re-established and memorial blood sacrifices will be offered (Ezekiel 43:15ff).

Therefore, the priesthood which began with Melchizedek in Genesis 14 will of necessity continue throughout the ages for God's ongoing plan of redemption requires His mediators to be present continually in order that His glory through His Son's redemption of men can be known upon earth:
"Then saith He unto His disciples, The harvest truly is plenteous, but the laborers are few; **_Pray ye_** *therefore the Lord of the harvest, that He will send forth* **_laborers_** *into His harvest."* (Matthew 9:37-38)

The Lord is focusing upon the great abundance of souls **_ready for harvest_**, but the laborers or practicing priests unto God who can and will actually reap His harvest are few!

He commands His disciples to pray as priests unto God laying the necessary groundwork in order for the Lord to call the laborer/priests He so desperately needs at this very moment in time and the coming *"time of the end"*.

Priesthood Practices of Melchizedek:
1. Supplied physical needs/refreshment-bread/wine (Genesis 14:18)
2. Supplied spiritual blessing to Abraham (Genesis 14:19)
3. Supplied opportunity for Abraham to worship the most high God through tithing (Genesis 14:20)
4. Gave the "most high God" the glory for Abraham's miraculous victory (Genesis 14:20)

This man Melchizedek spoke only a dozen words or so in the KJV text, but the impact he has had on the rest of Scripture is very significant for in this single appearance in the Word of God he laid down principles that continue on to this very day for every believer-priest unto God.

If we use just the activities listed above we can structure a very effective ministry to those that the Lord brings into our path. We as mediators between God and man can supply the physical needs of those brethren who engage in spiritual/physical warfare and are in need of both physical and spiritual nourishment.

Secondly, we must supply others with the spiritual blessings of the Lord Jesus Christ through our witness/testimony. We must be ready to answer every man that asks a reason of the hope that is in us and supply them with the answers necessary for the lost to be saved and be a blessing and encouragement to those who are in Christ.

Melchizedek was careful to give the glory to *"the most high God"* Who was responsible for bringing about Abraham's miraculous military victory when he concluded:
"And blessed be the most high God, who has delivered thine enemies into thy hand." (Genesis 14:20)

The Practice of the Believer-Priest unto God
It is the high calling and duty of every born-again priest unto God to offensively engage in the spiritual battle that rages in the

heavenlies against the *"principalities...powers...the rulers of the darkness of this world against spiritual wickedness in high places" (Ephesians 6:12)*. However, the only way actual victory can be attained is by *"putting on the whole armor of God" (Ephesians 6:11)*.

This is the last and possibly the most important *"put on"* command given by Paul in his inspired writings. He then supplies the believer-priest seven specific elements necessary for the soldier of Christ to be victorious in the battle. The first five are protective defensive armor and the last two are God's mighty offensive weapons.

Putting on the armor is a daily necessity for the child of God if victorious living is to be realized. The saint militant is the saint victorious, but this military struggle is not an earthly battle, it is waged in the heavenlies for the eternal souls of men who are battling the three progressive enemies of the soul, the world, the flesh and the devil himself!

And, just as soldiers on the battlefield must be disciplined, alert and capable, so also must the warrior in the Lord's army possess these military qualities in order to be effective in winning the battle for their Savior, the Lord Jesus Christ.

The one essential motive must be our love for Him recognizing we are an extension of His love to those to whom we minister. Love, therefore, is the prime mover in **all** of ministry that occurs when we pray mightily in the heavenly, moment by moment, Spirit-led battle that He lays before us.

It will be especially necessary to recognize, understand and utilize these spiritual warfare principles at the end of the age when Satan and his angels are cast down to earth inflicting upon faithful believers his *"great wrath because he knows that he has but a short time" (Revelation 12:12)*.

Paul outlines the foundational struggle in which each believer/priest must be engaged for we must never lose sight of the fact that we have been duly called as practicing priests unto God: *"For though we walk in the flesh, we do not war after the flesh; For the* *weapons of our warfare are not carnal but mighty through God to the pulling down of strongholds: **Casting down imaginations**, and every high thing that exalts itself against the knowledge God, and **bringing into captivity** every thought to the obedience of Christ: And having in a readiness to **revenge all disobedience**, when your obedience is fulfilled." (II Corinthians 10:3 –6)*

Notice, the three-fold mind control battle plan Paul outlines:
1. Casting down imaginations and every high thing that exalts itself against the knowledge of God
2. Bringing into captivity every thought to the obedience of Christ
3. Having in a readiness to revenge all disobedience

This letter was written about five years before Ephesians as Paul's continued understanding of the battle in the heavenlies progressively grew until he wrote the detailed account of spiritual weaponry given in Ephesians 6:10-18. That is where we find the specific *"weapons of our warfare"*.

The entire book of Ephesians must be understood as "The Book for the Battle" for Paul carefully unfolds the Lord's battle plan for each progressive enemy of the soul:
1. The World (Ephesians 1:1-3:21)
2. The Flesh (Ephesians 4:1-6:9)
3. The Devil (Ephesians 6:10-18)

Ephesians 6:10-18 is one of the most powerful and important passages of Scripture for the victorious Christian. That is, the Christian who is truly living in victory for the Lord Jesus Christ by winning the daily battle with the world, the flesh and the devil.

These vicious enemies of the Christian can not be defeated without God's formula for victory found in the book of Ephesians. In Ephesians 6:10, 11 Paul summarizes the entire book of Ephesians by dividing it into three specific areas. These three distinct divisions are especially designed by the Lord to give us the victory over the three enemies of our soul.

The first enemy is the world system and for this enemy Paul commands: *"Be strong in the Lord..."* literally: *"be continually strengthened in the Lord".*

This phrase summarizes chapter 1:1-3:21 as Paul gives us the ammunition to have complete victory over the allurement of the world system and all its trappings by knowing our present and eternal position in the Lord as described in these first three chapters of this powerful epistle..

The key word for victory over this first progressive enemy, the world, is *"faith"*:
"For whatsoever is born of God overcomes the world: and this is the victory that overcomes the world even our faith" (I John 5:4).

Faith based upon exactly who we are in Christ! Paul uses the phrase *"in Christ"* over 30 times in the book of Ephesians. Our heavenly position and possessions are thoroughly described in Ephesians 1-3 and beautifully pictured in Ephesians 2:6:
*"And hath raised us up together, and made us to sit together in heavenly places **in Christ Jesus".***

This is our **present** exalted position! We are "right now" supernaturally raised from being dead in our sins and seated in the heavenlies in Christ with all of the:
*"Spiritual blessings in heavenly places **in Christ**."(Ephesians 1:3)*

Faith in our position, who we are in Christ, and our possessions, what He has given us, are blessings that are eternal and will never change! We must rejoice in these manifold spiritual blessings for there are at least two dozen mentioned in these first three chapters of Ephesians:

1. He hath CHOSEN us in Him (Ephesians 1:3): Selected for Himself, Separated from the rest of mankind, Picked out from among many. Illustr: Abraham (Genesis 12); Demoniac of Gadara (Mark 5); Samaritan Woman at the Well (John 4)-All Gentiles

2. Having PREDESTINATED us (1:5): To appoint from the beginning, To foreordain, To decide beforehand (Romans 8:29) and lay out a plan for each believer/priest

3. The ADOPTION of children (1:5): The act of making us His children accomplished by His own will, giving Gentiles the same relationship to God as the Israelites (Romans 8:15; Gal 4:5)

4. He hath made us ACCEPTED in the Beloved (1:6): To make graceful, charming, lovely, and agreeable; To compass or surround with blessing and favor by enduing believer/priests with His grace.

5. In Whom we have REDEMPTION through His Blood (1:7): To buy back, ransom, liberate by paying a price, He already owned us by creation, but we were sold into the slave market of sin through the transgression of Adam, He then purchased us with His Blood! (Hebrews 9:12)

6. The FORGIVENESS of sins (1:7): Released from bondage, imprisonment and given full remission of the penalty of sin through the gift of repentance and faith in His Blood (Luke 24:47; Romans 3:25)

7. Having made KNOWN unto us the mystery of His will (1:9): He has given us the privilege to know the mystery of His will concerning His gathering together in one all things in Christ.

8. We have obtained an INHERITANCE (1:11): A portion allotted and given to the rightful heirs, those who are in Christ are joint-heirs with Him (Romans 8:17)

9. Ye were SEALED with that Holy Spirit of promise (1:13): To stamp permanently as a sign of ownership; To set a seal upon; To mark with a seal for security by the Owner

10. The REDEMPTION OF THE PURCHASED POSSESSION (1:14): To keep safe, secure, to purchase for oneself and preserve for a future day, The guarantee of glorification/glorified body is given by the indwelling Holy Spirit's presence.

11. To have THE EYES OF OUR UNDERSTANDING ENLIGHTENED (1:18): The spiritual eyes of the heart illumined to experientially know: 1. What is the hope of His calling 2. What the riches of the glory of His inheritance 3. What is the exceeding

greatness of His power:
Illustration: (II Kings 6:17) The eyes of Elisha's servant were opened

12. He hath QUICKENED us (2:5): To be made alive spiritually, To be energized with the life of God

13. He hath MADE US SIT TOGETHER IN HEAVENLY PLACES IN CHRIST JESUS (2:6): Our present position in the eyes of God is in heaven in Christ, just as Christ is in us here on earth in us, we are in Him in heaven! (John 15:4)

14. We are His WORKMANSHIP created in Christ Jesus (2:10): His work of art, His poem of love (Greek word for workmanship)

15. We are MADE NIGH by the Blood of Christ (2:13): To be brought near, to be ushered into the very presence of God before His heavenly throne i.e. *'the throne of grace' (Hebrews 4:16)*

16. The Lord Jesus Christ is our PEACE (2:14-17): Peace is not the absence of outer turmoil, trial, tribulation, but the presence of inner rest in Christ Jesus (John 16:33) regardless of circumstance.
"The peace of God which passes all understanding shall keep your hearts and minds through Christ Jesus." (Phil 4:7)

17. For through Him we both have ACCESS unto the Father (2:18): The act of bringing someone into the presence of an exalted dignitary or person of power, bringing a peasant into the King's court.
"We have access by faith into this grace wherein we stand"
(Romans 5:2)
"In Whom we have boldness and access by the faith of Him with confidence" (Ephesians 3:12)

18. Now, therefore, ye are...FELLOWCITIZENS (2:19): The reality of possessing citizenship the same as others who were natural born. The Gentiles brought into the same position as the Jew

19. Ye also are an HABITATION OF GOD through the Spirit (2:22): To be built together with others to make up the whole. All parts/pieces required to make up the entire Kingdom of God, God's dwelling place in His saints

20. That the Gentiles should be FELLOW HEIRS (3:6): To be joint participants in the blessing of the Jews *"Heirs together of the grace of life" (I Peter 3:7)*

21. That the Gentiles should be...PARTAKERS OF THE PROMISES (3:6): To be joint participants of the O.T. promises of the Jews

22. We take part in God's ETERNAL PURPOSE (3:9-11): God demonstrates to the principalities and powers in heavenly places His wisdom BY THE CHURCH, through Meditation on the Word, Spirit-led Prayer, Preaching of the Word, Witnessing with the Word and Winning of the Lost.

23. We have BOLDNESS, and ACCESS, with CONFIDENCE by the faith of Him (3:12): God gives a Fearless Confidence, Freedom to speak the Word, Courage with Cheerfulness, and an over-coming Christ-like Assurance to His children.

24. That He would grant you according to the RICHES OF HIS GLORY (3:16-19): Supernatural Spiritual Strength, The Knowledge of the Indwelling Presence of Christ, Being Rooted and Grounded in THE LOVE, Supernatural Comprehension, to experientially KNOW THE LOVE OF CHRIST, that ye might be filled with ALL the FULLNESS OF GOD!

Full comprehension of our position and possessions as completely described in the above list is a must for victory over the *"world"*. When the world and all its allurements knocks on the door of your soul, focus your heart upon the eternal spiritual blessings/possessions found in Christ and turn your desires and passions to these heavenly things (Colosssians 3:1). This will build your faith and provide complete victory over the sin of hungering and thirsting after **the things of this present world.**

Rejecting these temporal worldly desires by memorizing and meditating on the reality of these marvelous eternal blessings in Christ is the only answer for victory over the world!

Yes, it is our faith, faith rooted and grounded in our exalted unchanging, and eternal heavenly position and possessions that gives

us the victory over the world!
"For whosoever is born of God overcomes the world: and this is the victory that overcomes the world, even our faith." (I John 5:4)

The next progressive enemy Paul deals with is the animal who dwells within us who wars with the Spirit call the *"flesh"*. For victory in the battle with the flesh Paul commands: *"Be strong...in the power of His might"*. This precise and pointed command summarizes chapter 4:1-6:9. The expanded translation literally says: "being continually strengthened in the power of God's might".

This can be found only in the Person and work of the Holy Spirit. Five times in this section of Scripture Paul uses the word *"**walk**"* to describe our practical victory over the *"flesh"* by walking in the power of the Holy Spirit.

First of all, he commands every believer to: *"**walk** worthy of the vocation wherewith ye are called" (Ephesians 4:1)*. A worthy "***walk***" can only be accomplished by the Person of the Holy Spirit for Jesus said: *"Without Me ye can do nothing" (John 15:5)*.

We can not in the strength of the flesh, our own will power or vain efforts, please God:
"So then, they that are in the flesh can not please God" (Romans 8:8)

Only the Spirit of Jesus can please God! Only as we yield by faith to the power of the Holy Spirit will be able to *"walk"* with our Lord demonstrating the worthiness of our high and holy "*vocation*".

The primary calling that He has given us is to be Holy Spirit led priests unto God! And, this calling can only be accomplished as we obey this essential command:
*"This I say then, **walk** in the Spirit and ye shall not fulfill the lust of the flesh" (Galatians 5:16)*.

The second *"**walk**"* Paul emphasizes is found in (4:17) where he commands us to *"**walk** not as other Gentiles **walk**"*. He then describes a multitude of flesh works in (4:17-19) second only to his list in Galatians 5:19-21.

The only possible way to have victory over these flesh works described here is by faithfully yielding to the control of the Holy Spirit. This must be accomplished by faith on a daily basis when we prepare our hearts to enter the kingdom/battle in the heavenlies!

Being *"continually strengthened in the power of His might"* necessitates a full dose of the Word of God! We must digest the "living Word" by letting it *"dwell in us richly" (Colossians 3:16).*

The result of memorizing and meditating on the Word of God will result in Colossians 3:16 *"teaching and admonishing one another in psalms and hymns and spiritual songs, singing with grace in your hearts to the Lord."*

This is the direct result of letting the Word dwell in us richly! It is also the direct result of being *"filled with the Spirit"! (Ephesians 5:18, 19)* which are the key verses in this second section of Ephesians.

It is significant fact of Scripture that being filled with the Holy Spirit causes the same result as letting the Word of Christ dwell in us richly:
"Speaking to yourselves in psalms and hymns and spiritual songs, singing and making melody in your hearts to the Lord."
(Ephesians 5:19)

These two passages (Ephesians 5:18,19; Colossians 3:16,17) clearly underline the vital need of digesting/internalizing the Word of God in order for the Holy Spirit to fill and empower the believer for the victory to be won in the heavenly battle.

The third **"walk"** mentioned is in (5:2) where Paul gives still another command:
Walk *in love as Christ also hath loved us and hath given Himself for us an offering and a sacrifice to God for a sweet smelling savor."*

This command brings to mind the Lord Jesus' merciful love that only He could have demonstrated to us by His great suffering on the Cross. But it is this same supernatural love for Him that enables us to also *"crucify the flesh" (Galatians 5:24)* providing the opportunity to *"walk in love"* by His Holy Spirit.

We as lowly men and women could never perform such an act as this in our own strength. But, if we are *"continually strengthened in the power of His might"* we can actually *"crucify the flesh"* and *"walk in love"* as Christ walked (I John 2:5, 6) or else the command to do it would never have been given!

What a miraculous thought! We have the ability to walk in love as He walked if we *"present our bodies a living sacrifice"*(Romans 12:1) to Him who alone can do these miraculous works through us by the power of the Holy Spirit! The simple act of yielding to Him is all it takes…He does the rest!

The fourth *"walk"* continues to challenge us to give full control to the Holy Spirit as Paul gives still another command: *"Walk as children of light" (5:8)*. Immediately following he underlines the necessity of demonstrating the *"fruit of the Spirit"* in order to fulfill this most important requirement.

His emphasis centers on separating from all *"unfruitful works of darkness"* in the process we should do the positive thing and *"reprove them."* Here again the power and presence of the Holy Spirit is the means necessary to have the victory of walking as children of light.

The fifth and final *"walk"* Paul commands us to perform is found in 5:15:
"Walk circumspectly, not as fools, but as wise" which directly leads into the closing passage of this section dealing with the second progressive enemy of our soul the *"flesh"*.

This command is connected with wisdom and *"understanding what the will of the Lord is."* Unless we are filled with the Holy Spirit where all wisdom dwells, providing us with His full knowledge of God's will, we cannot expect to *"walk"* as we are commanded!

In order to bring the Holy Spirit's power into our lives we must digest the precious Word of God, allowing it to dwell in us richly providing the spiritual food/power the Holy Spirit thrives on.

It is through this process of memorizing and meditating on the Word of God that we are able to, by faith, yield full control to the

Holy Spirit allowing Him to *"sing psalms and hymns and spiritual songs, making melody in our hearts to the Lord"* and thereby get the victory over the *"flesh".*

The ultimate command given by Paul in this vital section for victory over the *"flesh"* is the most important: *"Be not drunk with wine wherein is excess, but be (continually) filled with the Spirit."*

The result of the Holy Spirit's filling is not speaking in tongues, but *"speaking to yourselves in songs and hymns and spiritual songs, singing and making melody in your hearts to the Lord".* Herein lies the formula for victory! As mentioned before, this result coincides with the Word of Christ dwelling in us richly!

Please compare these two passages: Ephesians 5:18, 19 & Colossians 3:16,17. If you want to be filled with the Spirit get filled with the Word! Allow the Living Word, the Son of God to control your mind, and the Holy Spirit will control your heart attitudes and actions! Besides, it's the only Biblical formula for God's success and prosperity! (Joshua 1:8; Psalm 1:2, 3; I Timothy 4:15)

All of these flesh-victory **"walks"** given by Paul can be handily summarized in one verse:
"But put ye on the Lord Jesus Christ and make not provision for the flesh to fulfill the lusts thereof" (Romans 13:14)

Paul's third summary command deals with the final and most deceptive enemy of our soul, the devil himself! He gives us the only sure-fire way for victory over the wily, wicked methods of the devil when he says:
"Put on the whole armor of God that ye may be able to stand against the wiles of the devil"(Ephesians 6:11).

It is this powerful spiritual weaponry, the full and complete armor of God centered in the Person of the Lord Jesus Christ that will give us victory over the *"wiles of the devil".*

This third command summarizes the closing section of the book of Ephesians: 6:10-18:
"Put on the whole armor of God, that ye may be able to stand against

the wiles of the devil. For we wrestle not against flesh and blood, but against principalities, against powers, against the rulers of the darkness of this world, against spiritual wickedness in high places."

With this powerful enemy of our soul we must *"stand against"* him, *"resist him steadfast in the faith" (I Peter 5:9), "resist the devil and he will flee from you" (James 4:7)*. All three of these significant commands of Scripture are rooted in the same Greek word meaning "to take a position in the battle, to oppose, to fight in a great struggle".

We must recognize beforehand that the devil seeks to open "Doorways" to our soul by entangling us in sins that provide him with the opportunity to "set up shop" (Ephesians 4:27) in our lives, thereby defeating us in the battle for souls.

These "Doorways of the Devil" are specifically underlined in the Word of God. The first is found in Acts 5:1-11, which records the sad story of Ananias and Sapphira. *"Satan filled"* the hearts of this couple *"to lie to the Holy Ghost"*. This sin of hypocrisy caused God to take the lives of both Ananias and Sapphira as demonstrations of God's chastisement of sin.

The Spirit of Hypocrisy involves putting on a mask, hiding the truth from others, trying to impress the saints by lying openly to the Spirit of God who was mightily evident in His working in the church at Jerusalem. Their penalty for yielding to the Spirit of Hypocrisy was instant physical death.

God exacted the degree of His penalty to the same degree His presence and power was manifested to these two believers who had experienced all the miraculous working of the coming of the Holy Spirit, the phenomenal occurrences of the day of Pentecost, the presence and power of the Apostles, witnessing the multitudes that were being saved, seeing God shake the building wherein they prayed, and the other unwritten acts of the Holy Spirit's power must have been very inspiring to witness.

But, they decided to yield to Satan and lie to the Holy Spirit. In the process they both lost their lives after their sin against the Holy Spirit was uncovered! The Spirit of Hypocrisy, the most often condemned sin in Scripture, is one of the easiest to fall into.

The second doorway to the devil's working is opened in II Corinthians 2:10, 11:
"To whom ye forgive any thing, I forgive also: for if I forgive any thing, to whom I forgave it, for your sakes forgave I it in the person of Christ; Lest Satan should get an advantage of us; for we are not ignorant of his devices."

Here Paul openly tells us that the sin of yielding to the Spirit of Unforgiveness literally opens the door to Satan and his deceptive devices, his crafty methods, and his spiritual trickery! If we are unwilling to forgive others Jesus clearly warns: *"neither will your Father forgive your trespasses."(Matthew 7:15)*

"And his lord was wroth and delivered him to the tormentors" (Matthew 18:34) is how Jesus describes the punishment that comes to those who will not forgive:
"So, likewise shall my heavenly Father do also unto you, if ye from your hearts, forgive not every one his brother their trespasses." (Matthew 18:35)

The word *"tormentors"* in v.34 literally means torture by use of the rack, to vex with grievous pains. This vicious abuse of the unforgiving person is not performed by the God of heaven, no, He simply allows you to be delivered to Satan and he does his all too familiar but torturous handiwork!

The third doorway is mentioned in Ephesians 4:26, 27:
"Be ye angry and sin not, let not the sun go down upon your wrath; Neither give place to the devil." The sin of wrath, outbursts of uncontrollable anger or rage, opens up a place for the devil to operate in our lives!

Paul says righteous anger is not sin, but allowing the sin of uncontrollable anger, wrath or rage to continue, letting the sun go down upon it day by day does indeed give opportunity for the wicked one to do business in and through the saint of God.

Yielding to the Spirit of Wrath is not an uncommon doorway

opened to the devil in the lives of God's people. Paul mentions this same word in his list of *"works of the flesh"* in Galatians 5:20 proving that this too was one of the many sins that was found there in the church at Galatia.

This very attitude yields control to the one who relishes the manipulation of God's children, in order that he might damn and destroy the testimony of those for whom the Lord Jesus Christ shed His precious Blood and died! Therefore, the believer must guard against this common sin or reap the Satanic consequences!

The fourth doorway opens in I Timothy 3:6: *"Not a novice, lest being lifted up with pride he fall into the condemnation of the devil."* The Spirit of Pride, was the very sin committed by the devil in the beginning causing his great fall (Ezekiel 28:13-17).

Pride is the root cause of the majority of man's sin. The attitude which causes us to think we are some great one or have accomplished some good thing in and of ourselves.

Thinking we, in our own strength and ability, are the ones responsible for something when, in reality, what have we gotten that we have not received? All good things come down from "The Father of Lights" the Lord God of heaven! There is nothing we can take credit for, nothing we in and of ourselves have accomplished.

This Spirit of Pride certainly opens the doorway to the devil's working in our minds, telling us lies that he *"the father of lies"* fabricates to deceive us! Three common signs of the proud are:
 1. Not giving God the glory for His working in our lives
 2. But instead taking credit for accomplishments
 3. Blaming others for failures.

The Bible lists at least seven devastating effects of the Spirit of Pride:
 1. Condemnation of the devil (I Timothy 3:6)
 2. Shame (Proverbs 11:2)
 3. Contention (Proverbs 13:10)
 4. Destruction (Proverbs 16:18)
 5. Deception (Jeremiah 49:16)
 6. Hardening of the mind (Daniel 5:20)

7. Resistance from God (James 4:6)

The fifth doorway to the devil is found in I Timothy 3:7: *"Moreover he must have a good report of those which are without; lest he fall into reproach and the snare of the devil."*

Falling into reproach refers to one who has blemished their testimony through openly committing sin. Our testimony is the most valuable thing we own and can not be purchased with money!

Therefore, if we continually sin and it is known by those *"which are without"* who are the lost, we will bring ourselves into *"the snare of the devil"*, the very trap he has set to cause us to be caught in our own sin!

This will surely cause those who are lost and saved alike to discount our words/witness thereby damning the souls of those that we could have impacted for the glory of God! Therefore, we, as children of God, must have a good report among all men if we are to witness and win souls for Jesus, otherwise the devil will claim another victory as we fall into his well-baited trap!

The last doorway of the devil is found in II Timothy 2:24-26:
"And the servant of the Lord must not strive but be gentle unto all men, apt to teach, patient, In meekness instructing those that oppose themselves; if God peradventure will give them repentance to the acknowledging of the truth; And that they may recover themselves out of the snare of the devil, who are taken captive by him at his will."

The Spirit of Opposition, actively opposing revealed truth, causing us to be hearers only and not doers of the word, deceiving their own selves plays right into the hand of the great deceiver himself! The Spirit of Opposition also rears its ugly head when we disregard and rebel against those whom God has put in authority over us.

This same Spirit of Opposition says: "I don't care what the Bible says I know what I've experienced" or "I will not separate from these worldly associations, music, friends, activities" or "Who does that preacher think he is, telling me what to do with my life?" or "It has been our tradition to...why must we change the way we always have done things, just because the Bible says..."

Those believers who actually oppose the revealed Truth of God oppose themselves, those in whom the Spirit of Truth abides, thereby causing them to fall into a trap, a snare specifically designed to take one captive coming under the power of the will of Satan himself!

The Greek word in this text indicates that this trap/snare requires outside help in order to be set free from the will of the devil which serves to underline the grave danger of opposing God's ordained authority.

So then, how do we enter into continual victory over the devil? By putting on the *"whole armor of God"*. How do we put on the whole armor of God? By *"putting on the Lord Jesus Christ" (Romans 13:14)* Who is clearly detailed and described here in the specific pieces of armor. It is an action of simple childlike faith! Through faith we must have *"our loins girt about with truth"* being protected by Him Who is Truth (John 14:6), the Lord Jesus Christ!

We must put *"on the breastplate of righteousness"* the very righteousness of the Lord Jesus Christ who is our Righteousness (I Corinthians 1:30).

Our spiritual feet must be *"shod with the preparation of the gospel of peace"* again through Him who is our Peace (Ephesians 2:14). Taking the *"shield of faith" "the faith" (Galatians 2:20)* found only in Him who is the Author and Finisher of our faith (Hebrews 12:2).

The spiritual *"helmet of salvation"* can only come through Jesus' salvation/deliverance for:
"Neither is there salvation in any other, for there is none other name under heaven given among men whereby we must be saved."
(Acts 4:12)

The next piece of weaponry is offensive. It is with the powerful, living Word of God that the soldier of Christ assaults the kingdom of darkness. Herein lies the weapon utilized for the putting on of all the armor of God:

"And take...the Sword of the Spirit which is the Word of God" (Ephesians 6:17b)

This offensive weapon is the very source of our faith, for *"Faith comes by hearing and hearing by the Word of God."(Romans 10:17).* Through it we gain all that is necessary to perform the supernatural fetes of faith in winning the battles with Satanic enemies for the Word of God does the work of God!

Just as the Lord Jesus Christ quoted the Word of God when tempted of the devil in Matthew 4:4, 7, 10 in order to refute and defeat the devil's temptations, so too, we must in like manner have the ability to use this most powerful weapon to do the same for:
"The Word of God is quick [living] and powerful and sharper than any two-edged sword, piercing even to the dividing asunder of soul and spirit and of the joints and marrow and is a discerner of the thoughts and intents of the heart. Neither is there any creature that is not manifest in His sight: but all things are naked and opened unto the eyes of Him with whom we have to do." (Hebrews 4:12, 13)

The second offensive piece of armor mentioned is the method whereby we commune with the King! Prayer, without it we would be still in our sin! It was the prayer of faith that brought us to the foot of the Cross, it was prayer that gave us the ability to cry out to God in repentance as we laid hold upon salvation by faith in what Jesus accomplished when He paid the penalty for our sin as He bled and died upon the Cross!

Prayer, the humble utterance of faith brought us to salvation and now brings us to Him who alone can save and deliver us from the presence and power of sin! Utilize the weaponry of God and walk in victory over the world, the flesh, and the devil and his manifold doorways of sin!

Paul gives precise instruction on exactly when to pray, what kind of prayer, how to pray, and who are the primary focus of the priest unto God's praying:
"Praying always, with all prayer and supplication in the Spirit, and watching thereunto with all perseverance and supplication for all saints." (Ephesians 6:19)

1. When? Praying **al**ways
2. What kind? Praying with **all** kinds of prayer and supplication
3. How? Watching and praying with **all** perseverance
4. Who? Praying for **all** saints

Although we must pray for those who are lost, prayer for the saints/brethren is the priority of the Holy Spirit-led believer-priest. This vital ministry is the overwhelming emphasis throughout the New Testament and should be the central theme of the militantly victorious priest unto God.

<u>Yes, the priest must be militantly victorious as a well-equipped soldier of Christ in the army of the King of kings</u>!

Paul made very specific provision in the epistle to the Ephesians, with definite and precise instruction in "The Book for the Battle" so that we might have complete victory over the three progressive enemies of the soul, the world, the flesh, and the devil.

However, the struggle that continues in the heavenlies against the devil and his angels will be at maximum strength during the last days of this age as Revelation 12 explains:

"And there was war in heaven: Michael and his angels fought against the dragon: and the dragon fought and his angels, And prevailed not; neither was there place found any more in heaven. And the great dragon was cast out, that old serpent, called the Devil, and Satan, which deceives the whole world; he was cast out into the earth, and his angels were cast out with him. And I heard a loud voice saying in heaven, Now is come salvation [deliverance] and strength [power] and the kingdom of our God, and the power of His Christ; for the accuser of our brethren is cast down which accused them before our God day and night. And they overcame him by the Blood of the Lamb and the word of their testimony; and they loved not their lives unto the death. Therefore, rejoice ye heavens, and ye that dwell in them. Woe to the inhabitants of the earth and of the sea! For the devil is come down unto you, having great wrath because he knows that he has but a short time." (Revelation 12:7-12)

The battle will intensify during those days and there will be those saints who overcome the devil as recorded in this passage. They will

utilize three important weapons:
1. The Blood of the Lamb
2. The word of their testimony
3. They will love not their lives unto the death

But, Revelation 13 gives another view of this same time period:
"And it was given unto him [the beast/Antichrist] to make war with the saints, and to overcome them; and power [authority] was given him over all kindred, and tongues, and nations." (Revelation 13:7)

Daniel provides these facts pertaining to this same time frame:
"I beheld, and the same horn [Antichrist] made war with the saints and prevailed against them...And he shall speak great words against the most High, and shall wear out the saints of the most High, and think to change times and laws: and they [the saints] shall be given into his hand until a time and times and the dividing of time."
(Daniel 7:21, 25)

<u>There will be those saints who overcome the devil and those saints who are overcome by the devil during the last days of this age.</u> Those who utilize the power of the Blood of Christ, have a blameless testimony and have sacrificially given themselves to the Lord even in the face of death will be victorious.

During this same time Daniel describes those who *"know their God shall be strong and do exploits. And they that understand among the people shall instruct many: they shall fall by the sword, and by flame, by captivity, and by spoil, many days. Now when they shall fall they shall be helped with a little help: but many shall cleave to them with flatteries. And some of them of understanding shall fall, to try them, and to purge, and to make them white, even to the time of the end: because it is yet for a time appointed." (Daniel 11:32-35)*

Victory does not mean deliverance from a martyr's death, but victory means facing death in the strength and power of the Lord Jesus Christ through His grace for there will be martyrs in abundance in that day. But, in order to be victorious we must be prepared for the battle by fully utilizing the Lord's spiritual weaponry.

This will be especially necessary for those 144 Thousand priests unto God who are called out to serve Him during the final days of this age and the ensuing Day of the Lord when planet earth will be a reeling cauldron of fiery and bloody judgment from the hand of God as described in Revelation 8-19.

These young Jewish men will be prepared to do battle with the devil and his emissaries during the time when he is cast down unto the earth which occurs right after the mid-point of the 70th Week of Daniel. They will be among *"they that understand"* described in Daniel 11:32-35 before they are sealed.

And, as *"the time of the end"* unfolds before our very eyes, it is certain that God will continue to bring to pass the events necessary to begin the 70th Week of Daniel through the restoration ministry of Elijah the prophet (Malachi 4:5, 6; Matthew 17:11), and the call and preparation of the 144 Thousand *"servants of our God" (Revelation 7:3)* who will make up **The Priesthood of the Apocalypse**!

The Purpose of God

The record in Scripture is clear, God has never left, nor will He ever leave His planet earth without a human witness to His great and glorious grace demonstrated by His redemption of men through the finished work of His Son, the Lord Jesus Christ, on the Cross.

Based upon this one single unwritten principle which is taught by example and precept throughout the written Word of God, from Adam through the 2,000 year history of the Church, it can be said that there will continue to be people of faith upon the earth, throughout the time of the end, the 70th Week of Daniel and the Day of the Lord.

As the previous messages have set forth, the 70th Week of Daniel, which God has determined upon His earthly people the Jews (Daniel 9:24), will also be utilized to purify the saints before they, *"the elect"*, are gathered by the angels (Matthew 24:31) and received into heaven (Revelation 7:9-17).

Before that magnificent event occurs, the Lord will call, prepare and seal 144 Thousand *"sons of Israel" (Revelation 7:1-8)* in order to provide the continuing testimony of His redemptive grace through the agency of redeemed men as He has chosen to do from the beginning of time itself.

While the Lord will call and utilize many different people to accomplish His end times purposes, these *"servants of our God" (Revelation 7:3)* are the focal point of "The Priesthood of the Apocalypse" for, when the Scripture is examined, it reveals that they are unlike any other group of believers ever to be set forth in the Word of God.

Their Redemption Ministry as priests unto God has been thoroughly planned and prophesied by the Lord as they will be His literal end times disciples *"following Him wherever He goes"' (Revelation 14:4).* They become the ultimate *"fishers of men"* according to Jesus own promise:

"Come ye after Me and I will make you to become fishers of men." (Mark 1:17)

Their task will be enormous as their great number indicates. For, at the beginning of this age the Lord chose, trained and sent out twelve disciples and they *"Turned the world upside down" (Acts 17:6).*

But then, during the end times, in order for His continuing purpose of redemption to be fulfilled, He has deemed it necessary to once again follow this same pattern of utilizing personal disciples.

He will not call and train a mere twelve disciples as in His first coming. He will need **_twelve thousand sets of twelve disciples_** to accomplish His great end times purpose of redemption. Their sheer number reveals the overwhelming magnitude of the ministry these young men will undertake.

It is imperative that the present-day Church of Jesus Christ recognizes its part in raising up these young men in order for the Lord to bring to pass His marvelous and miraculous plan.

The end of this age is closing in rapidly when He will most certainly come again just as He has promised in His Word (John 14:3; Matthew 24:30, 31) *"Even so come Lord Jesus" (Revelation 22:20).*

However, it is **after** He comes to resurrect, rescue, rapture, and receive the saints that these 144 Thousand Disciples of Christ will embark upon their most intensive Redemption Ministry.

Then they will carry the message of the Gospel of Jesus Christ (Daniel 11:32-35, 12:3) to those who also have been written in the Lamb's book of life (Revelation 13:8, 17:8).

There will be many that will *"**turn** from transgression in Jacob" (Isaiah 59:20)* and *"shall **call** on My name, and I will hear them: I will say, It is My people: and they shall say, **The Lord is my God**" (Zechariah 13:9).*

The unfolding of the lives and ministry of the 144 Thousand is indicated in Scripture as has been documented in previous chapters

In order to conclude these messages and clearly emphasize their great significance in God's plan for the time of the end, the following outline summarizes their future:

I. They are part of *"the remnant of her [the woman's] seed" (Revelation 12:17b)*
    *Time: The Middle of the 70th Week of Daniel
[Priesthood/Redemption Ministry]
  1. They are from the twelve tribes of Israel (Revelation 7:3-8)
  2. They are young men (Psalm 110:3; Revelation 14:4a)
  3. They are persecuted by Satan (Revelation 12:17b)
  4. They keep the commandments of God (Revelation 12:17b)
  5. They have the testimony of Jesus Christ (Revelation 12:17b)
II. They will *"know their God...understand" (Daniel 11:32-35)*
    *Time: During the Last Half of the 70th Week of Daniel
[Priesthood/Redemption Ministry]
  1. They shall be strong
  2. They shall do exploits
  3. They will have understanding
  4. They will instruct many
  5. They [some] shall fall, to try them, and to purge, and to make them white, even to the time of the end
III. They are *"the servants of our God" (Revelation 7:3)*
    *Time: During the Day of the Lord
[Priesthood/Redemption Ministry]
  1. They are sealed <u>before</u> the Day of the Lord judgments (Revelation 7:1-3)
  2. They are protected <u>during</u> the Day of the Lord judgments (Revelation 9:4)
IV. They *"shall be willing in the day of Thy power" (Psalm 110:3)*
    *Time: During the Day of the Lord
[Priesthood/Redemption Ministry]
  1. They are the time of the end priests unto God (Exodus 19:5, 6; Psalm 110:3; I Peter 2:5; Revelation 14:4, 5)
  2. They are the holy nation/time of the end Israel of God (Exodus 19:5, 6; Psalm 110:3; Revelation 14:4)
V. They will *"shine as the brightness of the firmament" (Daniel 12:3)*
    *Time: During the Day of the Lord
[Priesthood/Redemption Ministry]

      1. They are wise
      2. They turn many to righteousness
      3. They shine as the stars forever and ever
VI. They are *"with the Lamb" (Revelation 14:1, 17:14)*
      *Time: <u>During the Day of the Lord</u>
      1. At the end of the 70th Week of Daniel (Revelation 14:1)
      2. At the battle of Armageddon (Revelation 17:14)
VII. <u>They gather unto the King of kings populating Promised Land</u> (Genesis 49:10; Micah 5:3)
      *Time: <u>During the Millennium</u>
      1. Along with the Israelites who will be saved at the end of the 70th Week of Daniel (Isaiah 59:20; Micah 5:3)
      2. And faithful Israel, "the Woman" of Revelation 12 (Micah 5:3)

As God continues to unfold His plan, He will raise up this mighty army of priest/soldiers of Christ from the twelve tribes of Israel many of whom will likely come out of the families of the faithful in the Church of Jesus Christ (Revelation 7:1-8, 14:4).

The Gospel emphasis of the Lord Jesus Christ and the Apostle Paul: *"to the Jew **first** and also to the Greek [Gentile]" (Romans 1:16)* must now be the clear priority and compelling emphasis of evangelism in the present-day Church of Jesus Christ throughout the world.

In order for the Lord to return and bring this age to a close, these end times disciples of Christ must be called and prepared so that they might also *"turn the world upside down"*, fulfilling the plan of God for their lives and thereby exalt and glorify the Lord Jesus Christ.

But, the question arises: Just where will this great number of faithful Jews physically come from? The answer is: From across the earth, as alluded to in the following passages:
*"And after these things I saw four angels standing on the four corners of the **earth**, holding the four winds of the **earth**, that the wind should not blow on the **earth**, nor on the sea, nor on any tree. And I saw another angel ascending from the east, having the seal of the living God: and he cried with a loud voice to the four angels, to whom it was given to hurt the **earth** and the sea, Saying, Hurt not the **earth**,*

*neither the sea, nor the trees **till we have sealed the servants of our God** in their foreheads. And I heard the number of them which were sealed: and there were sealed an hundred and forty and four thousand of all the tribes of the children [sons] of Israel." (Revelation 7:1-4)*
*"And they sung as it were a new song before the throne, and before the four beasts, and the elders: and no man could learn that song but the hundred and forty and four thousand, which were redeemed from the **earth**." (Revelation 14:3)*

These verses give credence to the theory that the 144 Thousand will be called from throughout the earth. The *"four winds"* angels to *"whom it was given to hurt the [entire] earth and the sea" (Revelation 7:1,3)* were delayed from accomplishing their global mission of judgment until these young men were sealed, providing them with God's protection (Revelation 9:4) in the midst of His Day of the Lord judgment.

Notice, all four angels were delayed, not just the one angel who would bring judgment to the land of Israel where most of the world's present-day Jews reside. This great number of *"servants of our God"* will likely be called from across the planet being *"redeemed from the [entire] earth."*

As mentioned above, world evangelization of the Jews must be the clear priority of the church today, as it definitely was the focus of the Lord and the early church, including the Apostle Peter and the Apostle Paul. Even though Paul was unmercifully persecuted and soundly rejected by the great majority of the Jews during his ministry, he continued to go to their synagogues in each city attempting to win them to Christ (Acts 9:20, 13:5, 14:1, 17:1, 10, 17, 18:4, 19).

He was simply following his heart (Romans 1:15, 16, 10:1) and the emphasis that his Lord utilized during His earthly ministry. For, at the end of the Lord Jesus Christ's first coming, He gave this brief but vividly descriptive portrait of His public ministry:
"I spoke openly to the world; I ever taught in the synagogue, and in the temple, whither the Jews always resort; and in secret have I said nothing." (John 18:20)

In God's purpose there is coming a day, at the end of the 70th Week of Daniel, when *"the veil shall be taken away" (II Corinthians 3:16b)* from the spiritual eyes of His earthly people the Jews. Then, their *"Redeemer shall come to Zion, and unto them that turn from transgression in Jacob, saith the Lord." (Isaiah 59:20)*
"And so all Israel shall be saved: as it is written, There shall come out of Zion the Deliverer, and shall turn away ungodliness from Jacob." (Romans 11:26)

But at the present hour *"the veil is upon their heart"*
(II Corinthians 3:15) and the age-old methods used by the Lord Jesus Christ and the Apostle Paul continue to be the best ways to reach the Jews. They utilized Old Testament Messianic preaching: (Luke 4:15-21; Acts 13:16-39, 17:1-3, 18:28) and confrontational one-on-one evangelism: (John 3:1-21, 4:1-26; Acts 16:31, 18:4, 19:8).

In the purpose of God, it is the clear duty of the Church of Jesus Christ to pray for the Lord to send forth laborers into His harvest. They must focus their Holy Spirit filled soul-winning compassion upon the earthly people of God, the Jews, wherever they may be found as we close in on the Second Coming of the Lord Jesus Christ.

The time is drawing near when these young men, the 144 Thousand, will be called, prepared and later sealed for their Day of the Lord service to God. This great conversion of the earthly people of God may well take place during the powerful restoration/revival ministry of Elijah whom God will send (Malachi 4:5, 6) to His people.

He will of necessity follow the pattern of his two predecessors, Elijah and John the Baptist, preaching repentance and revival, *"Turning hearts... and restoring all things" (Malachi 4:5, 6; Matthew 17: 11; Mark 9:12)* in the process.

It is likely that the Lord will use this mighty prophet to also bring revival to the Church of Jesus Christ and spearhead the mass evangelization of His earthly people, including the 144 Thousand, during the first half of the 70th Week of Daniel. The 144 Thousand are given a unique title that points to this possibility:

*"These were redeemed from among men, being **the first-fruits unto God and to the Lamb**." (Revelation 14:4c)*

These young men appear to be the first Jews to be redeemed during the 70th Week of Daniel, which is the last seven years/week of the *"seventy weeks are determined upon thy people and thy holy city" (Daniel 9:24)*.

There will be many Jews saved later at the end of this restored *"holy covenant" (Daniel 11:28-32)* Jewish dispensation when the Lord intervenes as the completion of His first three purposes (Daniel 9:24) come to pass at which point in history:
"The Redeemer shall come to Zion…And all Israel shall be saved." (Isaiah 59:20; Romans 11:25, 26)

Before that day takes place the saints will experience the rise and rule of the Antichrist during Satan's *"great wrath" (Revelation 12:12) "the great tribulation" (Revelation 7:14)* which is the time just prior to the sealing of the 144 Thousand. The Lord describes this period of intense persecution:
"When ye therefore shall see the abomination of desolation spoken of by Daniel the prophet, stand in the holy place; (whoso reads let him understand) then let them which be in Judea flee into the mountains…For then shall be great tribulation, such as was not since the beginning of the world to this time, no, nor ever shall be. And except those days should be shortened, there should no flesh be saved: but for the elect's sake those days will be shortened." (Matthew 24:15, 21, 22)

The Antichrist will make *"war with the saints" (Daniel 7:21; Revelation 13:7)* pointing to the wholesale martyrdom of God's people which is also described in other passages:
"And they that understand among the people shall instruct many: yet they shall fall by the sword, and by flame, by captivity and by spoil many days…And some of them understanding shall fall."
(Daniel 11:33, 35)
"And when He had opened the fifth seal, I saw under the altar the souls of them that were slain for the word of God, and for the testimony which they held: And they cried with a loud voice, saying, How long, O Lord, holy and true, dost Thou not judge and avenge our

blood on them that dwell on the earth? And white robes were given unto them; and it was said unto them, that they should rest yet for a little season, until their fellow-servants also and their brethren, that should be killed as they were, should be fulfilled."
(Revelation 6:9-11)
"And when they [two witnesses] shall have finished their testimony, the beast that ascends out of the bottomless pit shall make war against them, and shall overcome them, and kill them."
(Revelation 11:7)
"And they [the brethren] overcame him [Satan] by the blood of the Lamb and the word of their testimony; and they loved not their lives unto the death." (Revelation 12:11)
"And I heard a voice from heaven saying unto me, Write, Blessed are the dead which die in the Lord from henceforth: Yea, saith the Spirit, that they may rest from their labors; and their works do follow them."
(Revelation 14:13)
"And I saw thrones, and they sat upon them, and judgment was given unto them: and I saw the souls of them that were beheaded for the witness of Jesus, and for the word of God, and which had not worshipped the beast, neither his image, neither had received his mark upon their foreheads, or in their hands; and they lived and reigned with Christ a thousand years." (Revelation 20:4)

This heinous slaughter of God's people will be cut off by the intervention of the Lord when He shortens/amputates this period called *"the great tribulation" (Matthew 24:21; Revelation 7:14)* which is authored by the Satanically energized Antichrist and his false prophet.

At that time the Lord will rescue *"the elect" (Mathew 24:22, 31)* when He comes in the clouds to rapture His church which is the closing event of this present age. But, before He comes, many Jews and Gentiles will die a martyr's death during this last and most severe holocaust of the people of God as is told to some of the martyrs of this same era:
"Rest for a little season, until their fellowservants also and their brethren, that should be killed as they were, should be fulfilled."
(Revelation 6:11)

When God's purpose is fulfilled for the *"great tribulation"*

(Matthew 24:21, 22), He will bring it to an end in His timing. He will send His Son, the Lord Jesus Christ, to rescue and gather *"His elect" (Matthew 24:31)* by rapture cutting off this vicious martyrdom of His people.

There will be three groups of believing Jews who will remain on earth to carry on the Lord's purposes during the Day of the Lord which immediately follows the resurrection, rapture, rescue, reception of the saints (John 14:3; I Thessalonians 4:13-18; Revelation 7:9-17).
1. The two witnesses prophesy during the entire last half of Daniel's 70th Week (Revelation 11:3-13)
2. The woman [Faithful Israel] is preserved during the entire last half of Daniel's 70th Week (Revelation 12:6, 13-16)
3. The 144 Thousand serve during the entire last half of Daniel's 70th Week (Daniel 11:32-35, 12:3, 10; Revelation 7:1-8, 9:4, 12:17, 14:1-5, 17:14)

One of God's priorities for His 144 Thousand disciples is the evangelization of His people. They will witness of their Messiah and His glorious grace to their brethren, the twelve tribes of Israel, preparing them for that day when *"all Israel shall be saved" (Romans 11:26)* at the end of the 70th Week of Daniel. Herein, is the primary purpose of God...The Grand Redemption of His earthly people.

This event has long been foretold:
"The scepter shall not depart from Judah, nor a lawgiver from between his feet, until Shiloh [The Lord Jesus Christ] come; and unto Him shall the gathering of the people be." (Genesis 49:10)

"And the Lord thy God will bring thee into the land which thy fathers possessed, and thou shall possess it; and He will do thee good, and multiply thee above thy fathers. And the Lord thy God will circumcise thine heart, and the heart of thy seed, to love the Lord thy God with all thine heart, and with all thy soul, that thou may live." (Deuteronomy 30:5, 6)

"And the Redeemer shall come to Zion, and unto them that turn from transgression in Jacob, saith the Lord. As for Me this is My covenant with them, saith the Lord; My Spirit that is upon thee, and My words which I have put in thy mouth, shall not depart out of thy mouth, not

out of the mouth of thy seed, nor out of the mouth of thy seed's seed, saith the Lord, from henceforth and for ever." (Isaiah 59:20, 21)

"Behold the days come, saith the Lord, that I will make a new covenant with the house of Israel, and with the house of Judah: Not according to the covenant that I made with their fathers in the day that I took them by the hand to bring them out of the land of Egypt; which My covenant they brake, although I was an husband unto them, saith the Lord: But this shall be the covenant that I will make with the house of Israel; After those days, saith the Lord, I will put My law in their hearts; and will be their God, and they shall be My people." (Jeremiah 31:31-33)

"Behold, I will gather them out of all countries, whither I have driven them in My anger, and in My fury, and in great wrath; and I will bring them again unto this place, and I will cause them to dwell safely: And they shall be My people, and I will be their God: And I will give them one heart, and one way, that they may fear Me for ever, for the good of them, and of their children after them: And I will make and everlasting covenant with them, that I will not turn away from them, to do them good; but I will put My fear in their hearts, that they shall not depart from Me. Yea, I will rejoice over them to do them good, and I will plant them in this land assuredly with My whole heart and with My whole soul."
(Jeremiah 32:37-41)

"For I will take you from among the heathen, and gather you out of all countries, and will bring you into your own land. Then will I sprinkle clean water upon you, and ye shall be clean: from all your filthiness, and from all your idols, will I cleanse you. A new heart also will I give you, and a new spirit will I put within you: and I will take away the stony heart out of your flesh, and I will give you and heart of flesh. And I will put My Spirit within you, and cause you to walk in My statutes, and ye shall keep My judgments, and do them. And ye shall dwell in the land that I gave to your fathers; and ye shall be My people, and I will be your God." (Ezekiel 36:24-28)

In the sure purpose of God, He will bring forth this great company of His servants, the 144 Thousand during this last "Jewish" dispensation, the 70th Week of Daniel. They will prepare the hearts of

His people in order to accomplish His continuing plan of redemption when the Lord Jesus Christ the:
"Redeemer comes to Zion, and unto them that turn from transgression in Jacob." (Isaiah 59:20)

As the outline [shown above] underlines the 144 Thousand's Day of the Lord Priesthood/Redemption Ministry, it is clear that they will undergo vital preparation during the time prior to their sealing when they will *"instruct...many"* who do not understand (Daniel 11:33).

They will be the Lord's life-line to His chosen people, the Jews, during the end of this age and the ensuing Day of the Lord for He will thoroughly prepare His servants for their time of the end Redemption Ministry as priests unto God when:
1. The Jews will be a *"people" (Daniel 9:24)*
2. The Jews will be in their *"own [promised] land"* (Deuteronomy 30:1-18; Ezekiel 36: 24-26, 37:21ff; Daniel 9:24)
3. The Jews will occupy/control their *"holy city"* Jerusalem (Daniel 9:24)
4. The *"prophet Elijah"* will be sent *"first"* to revive/restore (Malachi 4:5, 6: Matthew 17:11; Mark 9:12)
5. The *"holy covenant"* will be restored (Daniel 11:28-32)
6. The *"temple of God"* will be rebuilt (II Thessalonians 2:1-4: Revelation 11:1, 2)
7. The *"holy place"* included (Matthew 24:15)
8. The *"regular sacrifices"* will be offered (Daniel 8:11, 12, 9:27, 11:31, 12:11)
9. The Jews will worship in *"the temple of God"* (Revelation 11:1, 2)
10. *"The Sabbath"* will be honored (Matthew 24:28)
11. The sending of *"prophets"* to the Jews will occur (Malachi 4:5, 6: Revelation 11:3-17)
12. The tribal system will be restored as the twelve tribes of *"the sons of Israel" (Revelation 7:1-8)* will eventually be sealed

It appears evident that the Lord will bring to pass the same conditions that prevailed during the first 69 weeks of this prophesied time period during the remaining week or seven years, which is the 70th Week of Daniel.

At the present time [2009] He has already put the first three conditions into place. The Jews have become a people/nation, they have been in the land for well over a half-century and they have occupied their holy city Jerusalem for over four decades.

The next event on God's prophetic timetable appears to be the sending of Elijah the prophet for he *"truly shall **first** come, and restore all things" (Matthew 17:11)* referring to those necessary *"holy covenant" (Daniel 11:28-32)* conditions listed above.

That Elijah will be sent *"**first**"* before the Second Coming of Jesus Christ is underlined by this statement in the Apostle Peter's second sermon:
*"And He shall send Jesus Christ, which before was preached unto you: Whom the heaven must receive **until the times of restitution [restoration] of all things** which God hath spoken by the mouth of all his holy prophets since the world began." (Acts 3:20, 21)*

Just as certain orthodox Jews await God's sending of Elijah the prophet to this very day, so also should the Church of Jesus Christ look for the Lord to send this mighty Hebrew prophet who will *"turn hearts"* and *"restore all things"(Matthew 17:11; Mark 9:12) "**before** the coming of the great and dreadful day of the Lord" (Malachi 4:5)*.

This future sending of Elijah follows a previous pattern when the Temple and Jerusalem were destroyed in 586 B.C. Later the Jews returned to the land, rebuilt the temple, and eventually God sent the first Elijah-like prophet, John the Baptist, to His people before the Lord came to earth the first time.

The Lord Jesus then ministered on earth for 3-1/2 years which also points to the likely possibility of His influence/intervention on earth for the last 3-1/2 years of the 70th Week of Daniel starting with Micah 5:5ff when: *"This Man [Messiah] will be the peace when the Assyrian [Antichrist] shall come into our land: and when he shall tread in our palaces"*

This pattern is in the process of being repeated today for the Temple was destroyed in AD.70 and the Jews have become a people returning to their land and will eventually rebuild the temple. Then,

God will send the last Elijah-like prophet who will *"restore all things" (Malachi 4:5. 6; Matthew 17:11; Mark 9:12)* which will be followed by the Lord's Second Coming (John 14:1-3) when He:
1. Will be the Peace (Micah 5:5ff) 3-1/2 year ministry to the saints
   During the last half of The 70th Week of Daniel
2. Will rapture/rescue/saints (Matthew 24:30, 31; I Thess. 4:13-18;
   Revelation 7:9-17) Before The Day of the Lord
3. Will roar out of Zion (Hos.11:10, 11; Jer.25: 30; Rev.10:3)
   The End of The 70th Week of Daniel/Before Seven Last Plagues
4. Will redeem Israel (Isaiah 59:20; Romans 11:25, 26;
   Revelation 14:1) At The End of the 70th Week of Daniel
5. Will tread the winepress (Isaiah 63:1-4; Revelation 14:14,
   20, 19:11-15) The Battle of Armageddon
6. Will destroy Antichrist/Armies/Armageddon
   (Revelation 19:11-15) At The End of the Day of the Lord
7. Will physically reign for 1,000 Years on earth (Revelation 20:6)
   After (45) Day Restoration Period (Daniel 12:12)

In addition to the certain fulfillment of the above Bible prophecies, there will also be other major events taking place on the world stage in order for the 70th week to begin and the end times unfold:
1. The rise of the Antichrist/ *"king of the north" (Daniel 11:21ff)*
2. The economic/political growth/influence of Romanism
   (Revelation 17, 18)
3. The *"safety"* [peace] in the land of Israel (Ezekiel 38:8, 11)

As the Lord continues to prepare the Church of Jesus Christ, His people Israel and planet earth for His Second Coming and Day of the Lord judgment all of these things will definitely come to pass and thereby drastically alter the present-day [2009] complexion of planet earth.

These events will most certainly take place in God's perfect timing in order that His primary purpose is realized which is the loving redemption of those who have been written in *"the Lamb's book of life...from the foundation of the world"!*

Therefore, this very personal question must be asked:
"If you died today, are you **SURE** you would go to heaven?"

The Lord Jesus Christ made the requirements perfectly clear:
*"**Except** a man be born again [born from above], he cannot see the kingdom of God...**Except** a man be born of water [physical birth] and of the Spirit [spiritual birth], he cannot enter into the kingdom of God...Marvel not that I said unto you, Ye **must** be born again [from above]." (John 3:3, 5, 7)*

The Apostle Paul explained:
"For by grace are ye saved through faith and that not of yourselves it is the gift of God not of works lest any man should boast."
(Ephesians 2:8,9)
*"Testifying both to the Jews, and also to the Greeks, **repentance** toward God and **faith** toward our Lord Jesus Christ. (Acts 20:21)*

It is through faith that you are saved [born from above], faith in what the Lord Jesus Christ did for you on the Cross, for He lovingly shed His Blood to pay the penalty for your sin (Ephesians 1:7).

When you believe this truth [faith] and turn to Him from your sin [repent] and pray from your heart to **receive** the Lord Jesus Christ as your Savior, **then** you will be born from above by the power of God's Holy Spirit!

*"But as many as **received** Him, to them gave He power [authority] to become the sons of God, even to them that **believe** on His name."*
(John 1:12)

If you have prayed to **receive** the Lord Jesus Christ as your Savior, please contact us at www.btmi.org and we will send you Bible study information to help you grow in grace and in the knowledge of the Lord Jesus Christ.

THE AUTHOR'S BACKGROUND

-PERSONAL INFORMATION-

-Gloriously Saved March 7, 1980: Age 35
-Graduated from Bob Jones University (1986)
   Bachelor of Arts Degree:
     Major: Bible
     Minor: New Testament Greek
-Ordained: Independent Baptist / Bible Preacher (1987)

-MINISTRY EXPERIENCE-

-Local Church Revival & Evangelistic Meetings
-Prophecy Preaching /Teaching - www.prewrath.com
-Interim Pastor
-Adult Sunday School Teacher
-Tent Evangelism Ministry
-Rescue Mission Preaching & Discipleship Ministry
-Family Nursing Home Ministry
-Street Preaching Ministry
-Prison Preaching & Discipleship Ministry
-Internet Evangelism Ministry-www.btmi.org
-Truth for Truckers: Personal Soul-winning & Tract Ministry
-Author: "Raptured from Wrath", "The Practicing Priest unto God",
    "The Wise Woman of God" Booklets, Bible Prophecy Tri-folds,
      Eight Lesson Discipleship Series, Scripture Memory Plan,
       Gospel Tracts & Two Books: "The People of the Apocalypse" &
                       "The Priesthood of the Apocalypse"

-DOCTRINAL BELIEFS-

-The Verbal, Plenary Inspiration & Inerrancy of Scripture
-The Deity & Virgin Birth of the Lord Jesus Christ
-His Vicarious Atonement by the Shedding of His Blood on the Cross
-His Bodily Resurrection, Ascension, & Literal Pre-Millennial Return
-The Literal, Eternal Heaven for Saints & Literal, Eternal Hell for the Lost
-Salvation by Grace through Faith in the Shed Blood of Christ
-The Eternal Life [Security] of the Saints
-The Autonomy/Independence of the Local Church
-Biblical Separation from the World, Compromise & Apostasy

www.ingramcontent.com/pod-product-compliance
Lightning Source LLC
Chambersburg PA
CBHW031646040426
42453CB00006B/230